THE 7 STEP STARTUP
SUCCESS FORMULA

DR. ANU KHANCHANDANI

notionpress.com

INDIA • SINGAPORE • MALAYSIA

Contents

Contents

Preface

Hello and welcome.

I'm Anu Khanchandani

I am the founder of The Grey Cells - www.thegreycells.com. This organisation has been created with a purpose. Before telling you about the purpose I'll tell you a little bit about me.

I did my BTech in Computer technology in the year 1997. Thereafter I took the path that a normal software professional takes. I worked as a developer in Syntel (India). I moved on to the U.S. I worked with Delta Airlines in its Technology Division. I worked for around a year in Singapore with Reuters Asia where I took on a techno-managerial role as a Team Leader.

After having worked with all these CMM Level-5 companies, finally I felt the need to do something on my own and that is when I knew that I was bitten by the Entrepreneurial Bug! I started off by doing web development and digital marketing projects. I hired a team of developers who worked from various locations across the globe. I used to just coordinate with them on the phone and Skype. Got many such projects done by this team of virtual software developers and digital marketers. What was amazing about this setup was there were so many successful projects done, where I had never met the client since he was in Portugal, never met the developer since he was in the US and never met the marketer - well, even though she was in Pune but still away from Mumbai, so I never travelled till there!

So that is how I started off my entrepreneurial journey.

But later on as I went on gaining experience I realised that startups require a lot of consultation and hand-holding at each step of the way. That is when I started moving on to being a Business Consultant for Startups as a whole rather than just taking up projects for their product development and marketing. Also, I realised that there is a complete dearth of skills where managing the entire gamut of the Startup Business is concerned. Startup Founders knew what they wanted to do, but didn't know how to organise everything and go about it in a systematic manner. There was a clear need of honing their skills.

That is when I moved on to the next leg of the entrepreneurial journey and took up Training in addition to Business Consulting.

I set up a training institute (in those times when offline was the norm) where I used to partake in training for small batches of students. They came from various walks of life, all with one common goal - I have this idea and I want to launch a Startup. That was the most enjoyable part of my life!

And during this time I got an offer from Fintoo (formerly Financial Hospital) which is a Wealth Advisory company based in Mumbai where I was asked to provide consultation for Digital Transformation - moving on from legacy business processes to enabling them via IT processes. Taking something up from scratch, forming a team and creating a niche product www.fintoo.in has been my biggest achievement in my professional career. I realised that more than Digital Transformation it was actually giving birth to a new entity like a Startup. Now that I have a 40 member team to take care of the product and I have found the time to write this book I had been wanting to write for so long - I think I must've done something right to be in this sweet spot!

I have learnt so much in Fintoo in the past 7 years (and am still learning even though they call me the IT Mentor) that I felt the need to share these things with as many startups as possible so that I could see people converting their ideas into actual realities.

So that is where I also ended up creating a course called 7-Step Tech Startup Formula. The sole aim was that I could share this knowledge base with startups in a very organised way. I could of course train, I could consult, but considering the limited time and monetary resources that Startup Founders start off with I wanted to create a self-paced course which could be accessed at any time from anywhere.

This book is a textual conversion of the same course for those who are more comfortable reading rather than taking up an online video course. If you are interested in the video course it can be accessed at   https://thegreycells.com/wordpress-cms/product/startup-idea-to-business-plan-in-60-days/. The course has Templates for Pitch Deck , Business Plan and a lot more in case you are interested. The Bonus - where I provide a free online consultation for 30 mins to all Startup founders out there is also available for you - the reader of this book.

So dear reader, my heartfelt thanks for buying this book. Hope when you reach the end, you have a plethora of knowledge which can help you launch your Startup and convert your idea to reality. At any step if you are stuck , remember I am just a call/message away. Feel free to get in touch at www.thegreycells.com

Chapter 1

What Will You Have Achieved at the End of this Book?

I'm elated to have you here.

1. Because I feel happy for myself that I could convince yet another person to take the path of Entrepreneurship.

2. Because I feel happy for you that you have taken the right decision by deciding to take the first step towards your Startup Dream.

To start off with let me give you an idea about what we will be covering in this introductory section.

- Common Business Elements
  - All businesses have a set of common elements for which the artefacts need to be built.
- What will you have achieved at the end of this book?
  - Let's be very clear here. You are not here for just theoretical knowledge. You need to carry back something tangible to justify why you spent money on this book.

Common Business Elements

In 2018 when I decided to create a course for Startups based on my 25 years of experience. The sole aim was that I could share this knowledge base with startups in a very organised way. I could of course train, I could consult, but considering the limited time and monetary resources that Startup Founders start off with I wanted to create a self-paced course which could be accessed at any time from anywhere.

However when I shared this idea with colleagues and friends many of them told me "You can't teach someone how to build their business".

Well, I'll be very frank, that did put me in a doubt for a moment. Each business is different, each has its own challenges and strategies. So can I really teach someone everything that I have learnt in my experience with Startups.

I thought and I thought for days together just staring outside in the space sitting on my window sill.

Here is the answer that inspired me and encouraged me that I was on the right path.

Come to think of it, a Startup is just another business which is new, just like a baby is just another human which is just born. By categorising it in that way all we are doing is giving it a chance to be molly-cuddled and pampered till it takes off to be the next BIG thing. 😊

Agreed that every business is different, but

Every business needs a business plan which in turn describes its

- Value Proposition
  - What does it bring to the table and why should people buy from it rather than its competitors?
- Team Requirements
  - Who will help you build your Startup, how will you get them on board and what will be their roles and responsibilities?
- Business Financials
  - I am not asking you to be a CA here. All I am saying is every business needs to know what are its products/services, what is the value at which they want to sell each one of those, what will be their expenses and in the end what will be their PnL. Is the business even viable to be taken up?
- Product Strategy
  - When I say product here, I am talking about the presence that you create for your business on the internet. It could be a simple website or an app. Or for that matter, if you belong to the software domain, your product offering is an app itself which provides some benefit to the user be it productivity or finance or health or anything else.
- Marketing, Sales and Post Sales Strategy
  - With technology touching every sphere of a business, now your business can have a local, national or global reach via Digital Marketing techniques. Automation at each step reduces costs and Go to Market time and is the smart way to work in this century. Once you have a customer on board, gone are the days when you would have to set up a BPO office to take care of their needs. Tools have made it easy and convenient for both the customer and the customer rep to interact with each other and solve issues.

- Strategising these 3 aspects of a business and putting them in a business plan is a very important step that every business must take before it even starts manufacturing the product.

What will you have achieved at the end of this book?

I am not the only Business Coach around. There are many distinguished Business Coaches and Gurus out there. At the end of the day, our aim is not just to give you knowledge and jargon.

You are here for tangible outcomes in clearly defined steps to reach your milestones.

Here's to your success!

Chapter 2

Interesting Startup Statistics

In these testing times, all that a Startup Founder needs is a little encouraging pat on the back which says "If they could do it, you could too. So don't lose hope"

Here are chosen 10 interesting Startup Statistics which will cheer you if you already are OR are an aspiring Startup Founder.

If you are part of the Statistical graph, you have reason to cheer, if you are not there yet, you know what to do to get there.

1. Fastest growing Startup Sectors

[Source : www.startupgenome.com]

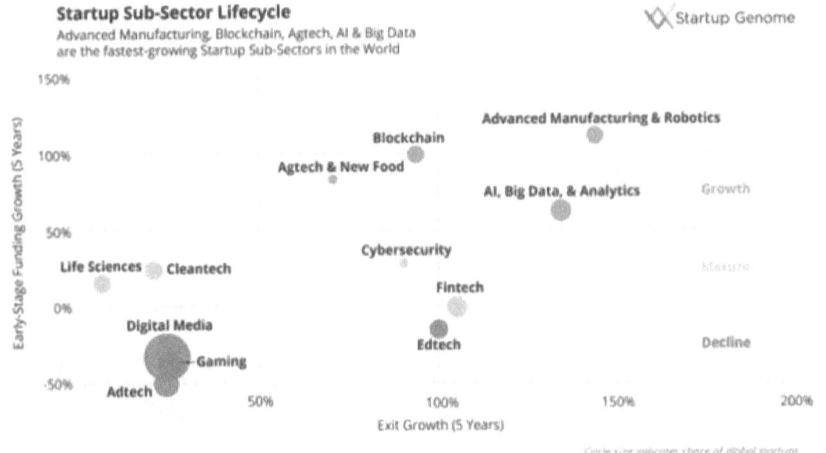

2. Common Reasons for Startup Failure

[Source : https://findstack.com/startup-statistics/#Startup_Failure_Rate_Statistics]

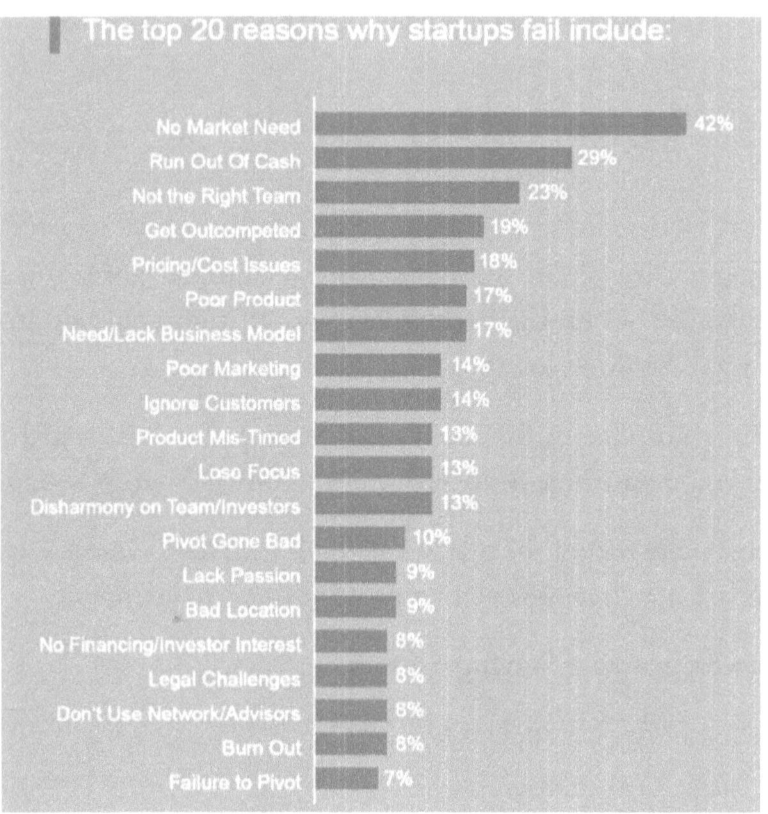

3. How India is encouraging Startups

[Source : https://economictimes.indiatimes.com/tech/startups/what-economic-survey-2020-21-says-about-indias-startup-ecosystem/articleshow/80586774.cms]

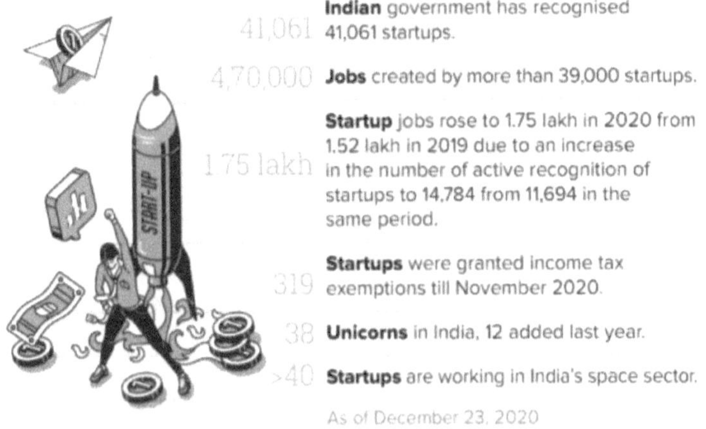

4. Who said Covid affected Indian Startup Funding badly?

[Source : https://economictimes.indiatimes.com]

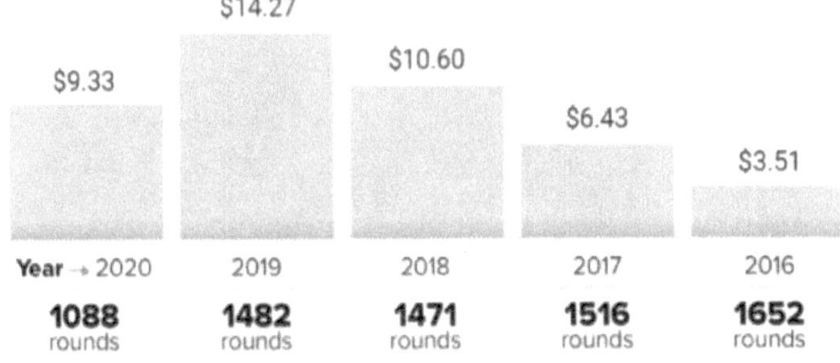

5. Unicorns who did India proud

[Source : www.statista.com]

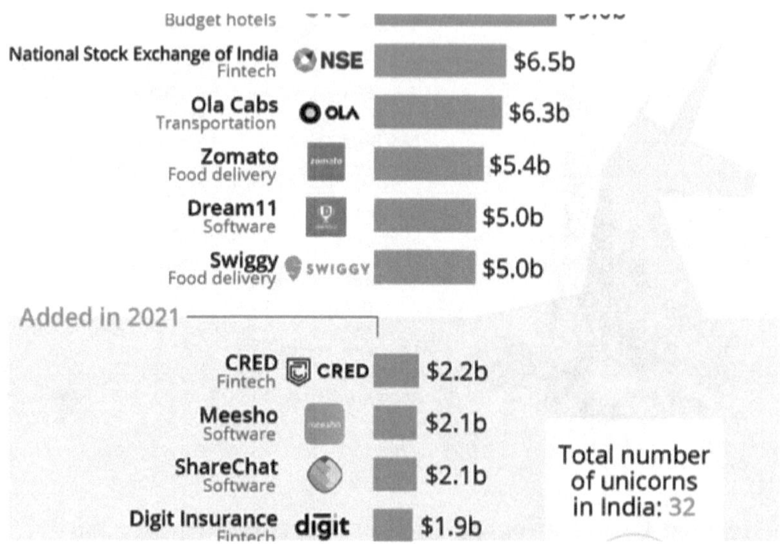

6. Startups raise nearly 3 rounds before they get to Series A

[Source : www.findstack.com/www.techcrunch.com]

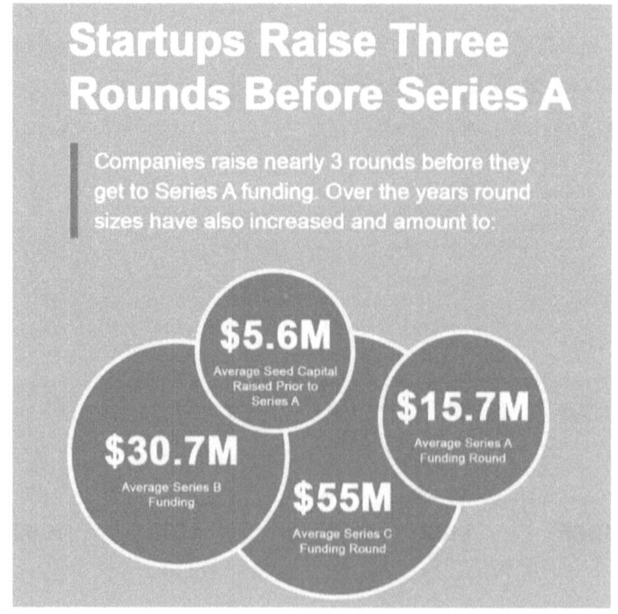

7. Watch out for these ECommerce Segments

[Source : https://economictimes.indiatimes.com/tech/technology/indias-e-commerce-sector-sees-big-growth-in-2021/articleshow/80055318.cms]

E-COMMERCE SEGMENTS TO **WATCH IN 2021**

Key Reasons For Growth

Online grocery
The entry of Reliance and Tata will spur competition

E-pharmacy
Consolidation in the sector and tailwinds from Covid-19

Social commerce
Increased VC investments and focus of giants such as Facebook

Direct-to-consumer
More brands investing in direct channels due to Covid-19 amid increased consumer interest

SUPER APPS *WHATSAPP'S INTRODUCTION OF PAYMENTS AND SHOPPING FEATURES WILL SUPERCHARGE THE INDUSTRY*

8. At what age are Entrepreneurs likely to find success?

[Source : https://insight.kellogg.northwestern.edu/article/younger-older-tech-entrepreneurs]

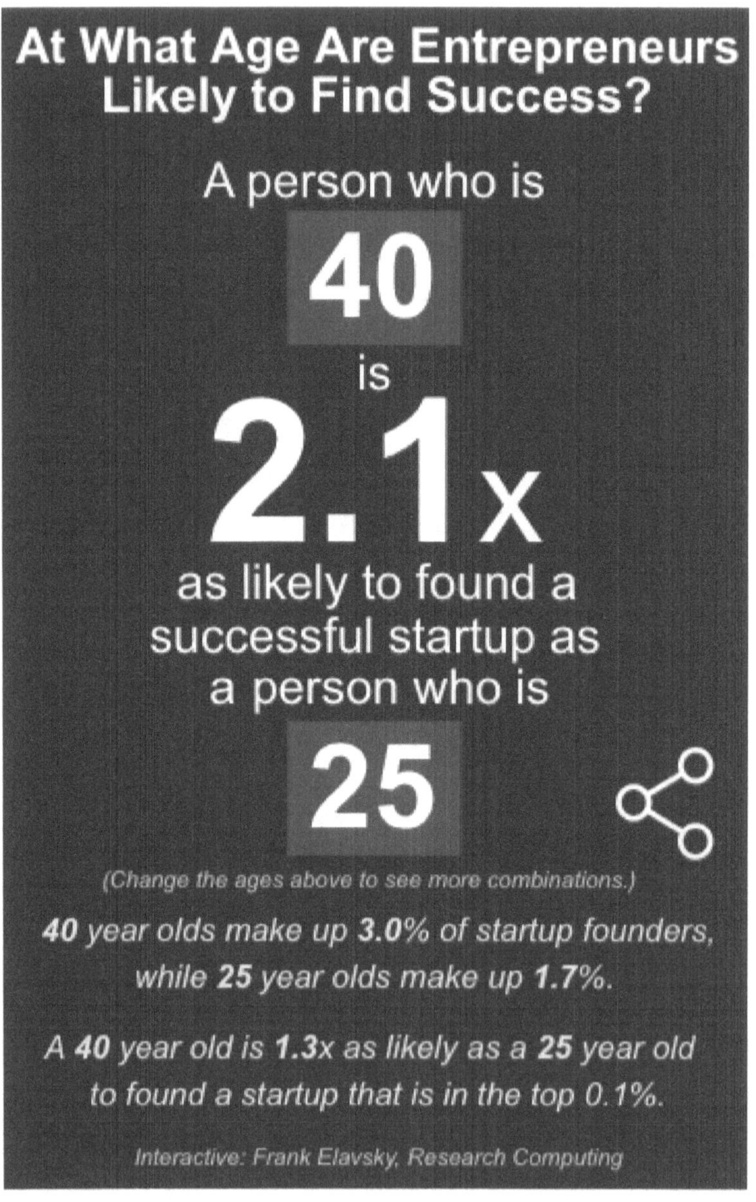

9. Top Skills required for Startup Success

[Source : https://lvivity.com/25-insightful-statistics-about-startups-for-2021]

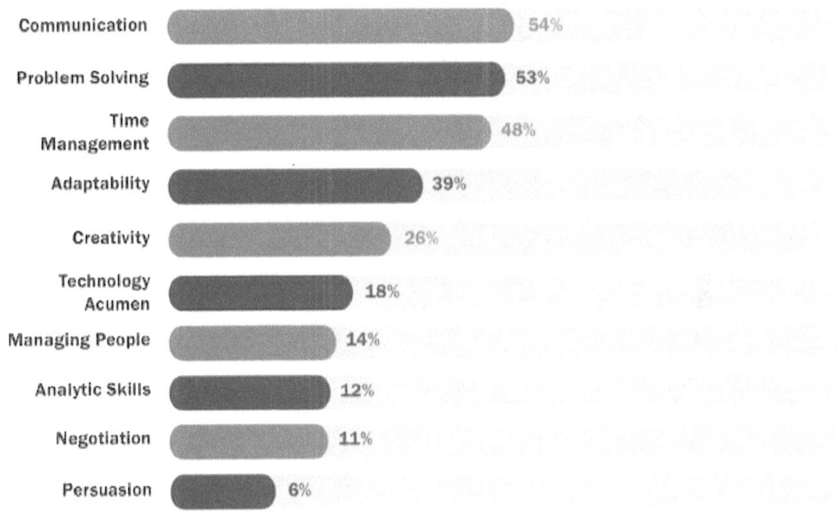

10. Women in Startups

[Source : https://www.guidantfinancial.com/small-business-trends/women-in-business/]

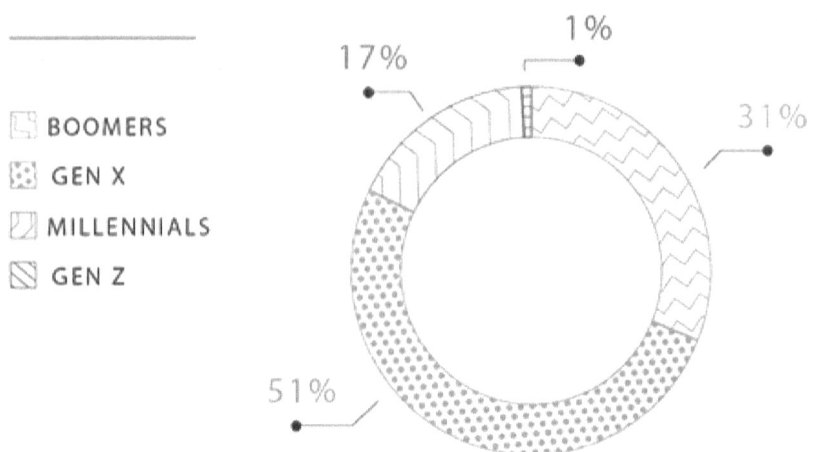

Hope I could spread some cheer and give you hope as a Startup Founder that all is not lost, just because there was a pandemic.

It's time to hold on to that cheer and move ahead in full speed towards realising your Startup Success Dream by following a clear proven 7-Step process that I have outlined for you in the upcoming topics.

Chapter 3

The Top 10 Reasons Why Startups Fail In their First Year

Don't worry about failure. You have to be right only once.
– Drew Houston, Co-Founder – DropBox

Failure is natural. Failure is good. It teaches you a lot as it happens. However, if you don't understand why it happened and don't bounce back from it – then it's the worst thing to happen. Based on what I have learnt in my 2 decades of experience as a solopreneur myself and having consulted many entrepreneurs – here is my list of Top 10 reasons why Tech Startups fail in the 1st year of their formation

Reason # 1: Hazy Vision

Chase the vision, not the money. The money will end up following you.
– Tony Hseih, Co-Founder – Zappos

It all starts with a dream.

It is this dream that takes the form of a defined vision. The vision doesn't strike at once. It evolves. Sometimes, over a long time. And that is absolutely fine.

Where most Tech Startups falter is, in discussing and documenting the vision in complete clarity. Many are not even aware that there is a complete process behind it.

The Vision has to be crafted in as much detail as possible. The larger the time the Founders spend on their Vision Documentation, the better the final product will turn out to be. You can't be in such a hurry to get to the market that you think spending too much time on the Business Plan is a waste.

The essential elements of the Vision Documentation which need to be brainstormed and chalked out are as follows :

- A Consumer Problem

- The Solution that solves the Consumer Problem

- Market Opportunity for the Solution – Why should you or an investor put their money in this?

- Competitor Research – Who and How they are doing it

- Software Development Plan – Prototype, Technology, Tools

- Marketing Plan – Modes and strategies of marketing (Offline, Online)

- Financial Plan – Money that will be needed to run the show and its sources

Again, this is just the tip of the iceberg. Delving deep into each of the above points and putting them down in Black And White is the key to making sure Reason # 1 is nipped in the bud.

Reason # 2: Dearth of Knowledge

I find it hard to manage somebody's work unless I have an
intimate knowledge of how to do it myself.
– Justin Kan, Co-Founder – Justin.tv

Tech startups are mostly a blend of 2 worlds – Technology and
the Core Domain which is being enabled by that technology.

Unless and until all the Founders have a knowledge of both
these important components things are not going to move in the
direction intended.

After all, learning is and should be a continuous part of a Startup
Founder's schedule. More so, if you are a Technology expert then
learning the Core Domain becomes mandatory and vice versa.

If there are hurdles in the mind of either or all of the Founders,
it will be a difficult game ahead since no one is going to understand
the point of view of the other.

Also, it is important to mention that just because you are a
Founder, doesn't mean that you don't have to understand the latest
developments in your field since you won't be doing the "groundwork".

To get the ground work done by someone, you need to know
the in and out of the implementation so that you can help when
needed or at least give a high-level view to make things happen.

Reason # 3: Underestimating Competitors

Pushing that last 5% harder than your competitor is so often the difference between success and failure.
– Sam Altman, Y-Combinator

There is enough space for everyone in the market. It's how well you do your thing than your competitor that gives you an edge over him/her.

But for that you need to know where they stand and for that you need to do some good amount of research.

Competitor research could involve many aspects. Few of them being – Product Feature comparison, Revenue Mode, Revenue Figures, Funding received, App Traction, Response Time, Marketing Strategies, Fan Following.

At the high level the above would suffice to start off with.

At a SEO (Search Engine Optimization) level you could also figure out what keywords they rank for. There is nothing wrong or unethical in doing this. It only helps you prepare better for your SEO strategy.

Reason # 4: Mutual Trust between Founders

Choose a Business Partner as carefully as you would choose a spouse!
– Emma Jones, Founder of Enterprise Nation

Trust is an important component of practically every relationship. More so in a business one! When 2 or more people come together to initiate a Startup most often than not it comes up as a casual idea.

Things then take a formal approach down the line and slowly work items start getting delegated as KRAs. And very rightfully so. There is nothing wrong with that.

One major reason for Tech Startups failing in their first year is core team clashes. Generally the clash is a lack of trust in the other person executing his part of the duties/KRA.

This is especially prevalent in Tech Startups for which the core domain is something else like EdTech, Fintech, HealthTech and so on. The person belonging to one domain doesn't understand the decisions made by the other.

It sounds blatant to say this but a better way would be to blindly trust your Co-Founder. If you found him/her worthwhile to start a venture with, then he/she better be worthwhile enough to trust blindly for the decisions related to his/her domain.

Even with widely different profiles, it is how well you gel with the others not belonging to your core field of work and how diligently you believe that whatever decisions they take will be for the well being of the company.

That is the bottomline in preventing any fallouts.

Reason # 5: Team Respect

Individuals don't build great companies, teams do.
– Mark Suster, General Partner – GRP Partners.

A collection of good people, each excelling at what they do is the key to any Tech Startup's success.

Good people are hard to find. You don't take a magnifying glass and start looking for them and they don't have a "good" label on their heads that you just pick them and make them start working.

When you undertake a recruitment activity, yes you define a Job Description document, you post the job, you interview people and take them on board if they satisfy your criteria. But do they all always stay back? Some will last in your company till the end of time, some will probably disappear on the next day.

There is a connection that is to be built with your team. And connection starts with mutual respect. No matter what the designation of the person whom you hire, it's how much you respect and trust that person to do his/her job that matters at the end of the day.

More importantly the relationship evolves in a stronger way when you take time and effort to mould them and to teach them so that they give you what you expect of them.

It takes a very strong team to create a sustainable business and there is a lot of effort that goes into it and it all starts with a basic level of respect.

Reason # 6: Zero Standard Operating Processes

85% of the reasons for failure to meet the customer
expectations are related to deficiencies in Systems
and Processes .. rather than the Employee
– W. Edwards Deming

Expecting anyone to give results without Standard Operating Processes (SOPs) is like telling him/her to complete a marathon without giving them the directions of the track on which they are supposed to run.

Just like Business Vision Documentation should be in Black and White, the company's SOPs also should be in Black & White. For every new joinee , they must be discussed and clarified so that they are adhered to the T.

To start off with some elements of a SOP for a Tech Startup could be outlined as follows. They could also be customised or tweaked as per your organisation, but the core thing is that they should exist and they should be implemented with discipline.

- Functional (Domain) Expertise Requirements
- Software Development
  - Guidelines
  - Tools
  - Portfolio
  - Release Plans
- Digital Marketing
  - Budgeting
  - Lead Analysis
  - Content Management
  - Physical Inventory Management
- Technical Support
- Training
- Back Office
  - Hardware
  - Vendors

- Accounts
- HR
  - Salary Processing
  - Recruitments
- Sales
  - Targets
  - Performance Monitoring
- Event Management

Reason # 7: Understanding Funding

That's the secret.
Convince yourself that your Startup is worth investing in,
and then when you explain this to investors,
they will believe in you.
– Paul Graham, Founder – Y Combinator

There have been Tech Startups who have applied for funding, just for the heck of it. They could have easily managed in a Bootstrapped way, but no! The fad is to get funded – Series A, Series B .. Series Z! They want it all.

And once it comes to them, they start strategizing how to spend it!

Not all Tech Startups need that kind of money. In fact, in the infant stage, no startup needs it. I would say, when you start an initiative, get your hands dirty with all that you can.

Chalk out the software development plan, get your hands dirty with content marketing. So what if it is not your field. Take up a course and do it.

Only then will you get an idea about what it takes to build all the elements of a successful business and only then will you understand the sweat and toil that goes into each activity that is needed to convert your vision to reality. And that's the only way to know how much money you need so that you can apply for funding.

Assessing this correctly will help you proceed in an organised and planned way rather than just jumping into it and seeing how much you can squeeze out because that is the in-thing to do.

Also remember at all points that more the investors in your company, more is the liquidity of your share. This is your dream, your vision and your sweat and toil has gone into it. Be frugal in giving it out.

Reason # 8: Unclear Pitching

For the most effective pitch, focus 80% on the
problem and 20% on the solution.
Dave McClure, Founder – 500 Startups

This originates from Tech Startup Failure Reason # 1 – Hazy Vision.

If your Business Vision Documentation is unclear, it is obvious that when you create a Pitch Deck, it will be a jumbled version of your thoughts.

I have seen Pitch Decks which even have a messed up Agenda – the first thing that you see when you open up the Pitch Deck is messy and it puts an investor off immediately.

Ok, here's the deal. A Pitch Deck is the simplest thing to create – provided of course, that your vision is clear. There are Pitch Deck templates available all over the web which have exactly the same elements which have been created after a lot of research with investors. Pick one up, fill in the blanks to the best of your capabilities and you are good to go! There is no rocket science there.

Reason # 9: Overspending/Underspending

Penny wise, pound foolish
– Robert Burton (Scottish Proverb)

A proverb that often comes to my mind when I see some Tech Startup Founders creating Annual Budgets.

A lavish office space is included on top priority but increasing a Software Developer to deliver software faster is considered an overspend! This is that category who doesn't know where to spend.

And then there is another category. Those who overspend because they have been funded. Hiring a Revenue Team with 15 people on board when 5 could easily do the job if you train them efficiently and give them the requisite process to meet their targets.

The frugal ones are actually a recommended kind. However, frugality to an exaggerated extent (sometimes when you would think twice before spending for an employee's well being) – well that kind of does more harm than good.

Knowing where and how much to spend is half the battle won.

Reason # 10: Lack of Persistence

I am convinced that half of what separates successful entrepreneurs from the non-successful ones is Perseverance
– Steve Jobs – Founder – Apple

Try, try till you succeed.

If you have a vision and you are convinced about its success then keep moving. Keep moving with your defined plan. Tweak the journey if the reality tells you so, but don't quit too soon.

I have seen some Tech Startup Entrepreneurs starting off with an exit strategy in mind. If that is the case then you would rather not go on that path.

Having said that, I will contradict myself a little by saying that if you know you have done your best and have exhausted all your mental and physical resources trying to make it happen but if you still don't see it budging – then sit back and take a call.

Don't quit too soon, but if you have a conviction that the time has come when you know you have given it your everything but dragging it beyond this would only deplete you of your peace of mind, then think about the possibility of a hand-over or a closure.

It's just about knowing the right decision to take at the right time.

Chapter 4

11 Tips to Maintain Your Sanity in the Startup Chaos

"You need chaos in your soul to give birth to
a dancing star"
— FRIEDRICH NIETZSCHE

Chaos is good. Chaos is desirable.

Sounds weird right?

Well, I have been taught to find the positive in everything. I find chaos a positive sign that things are moving. Chaos is an indication of absence of inertia. And that is good.

I started my journey as an entrepreneur, not out of passion, but out of need. A need to be there for my child in her growing years. And believe me when I say, nothing could be more chaotic than that. Developing a website for a client and managing a child was chaos at its peak.

But I managed. Not just managed. Enjoyed every bit of it! There were peaks and troughs for sure, but when I look back I don't feel an ounce of regret in deciding to embrace the chaos in the way that I did.

And here are my learnings lessons as an entrepreneur, for me it was motherhood at the side, for you it maybe some other challenge. What matters is maintaining your sanity, your zen through it all so that when you look back you feel pride and joy like I feel today.

1. Know your Why

Startups are not always born out of passion.

This was a new lesson I learnt from this amazing book by Cal Newport – "So good they can't ignore you".

My entrepreneurial journey did not start with passion. It started with a need. And there is nothing derogatory about that. Knowing why you are doing what you are doing, knowing why you chose the difficult life of an entrepreneur is half the battle won.

Once you are aware of the motivation behind the decision, you will survive its chaos.

2. Change is good. Be agile

I learnt this the hard way.

While working as CTO in Fintoo, I often asked the Board, "why do you change plans so often?". It was frustrating because I had to pivot the goals of the technology team with the changing plans of the company as a whole.

Along the way though, I started accepting it since some of those pivots at the right time, resulted in revenue and corresponding profits.

Having said that, I will be quick to add that agile is a very misused concept. Agility surely doesn't mean changing things at the drop of a hat.

Maintaining a healthy trade-off in deciding when to pivot and when to go on in the flow is a skill which comes only with experience. But once you master it, it is the number 1 way to handle chaos which comes with change.

3. Celebrate the small wins

Every step you take, is a step towards your success.

Giving yourself and your team a pat on the back for every small achievement will go a long way in keeping your Startup charged and will keep the adrenaline at its peak.

For that, it is important that you define your Minimum Viable Product (MVP) and work hard towards achieving the same in each phase of your product launch.

4. Cut your losses. Be frugal

As an entrepreneur, you have to have the conviction to keep the purse strings tight.

Marketing expenses especially tend to go out of hand. Here's a complete article on how you can balance out marketing expenses.

Also, a note of caution. Going to the other extreme where you find every expense unreasonable, would cause more harm than benefit.

A simple formula to use here would be to think about the benefit in terms of not just money directly but even time and energy sometimes.

5. Persist till it makes sense

We as entrepreneurs start with a dream. A dream to make it big.

A lot has been said about "Don't quit". And I support it. I support it with a pinch of salt.

Persistence and the patience to hold on is needed. Quitting at every small hurdle is not something that is advised.

However, at the same time I will be quick to add that knowing when to stop trying is something that every entrepreneur must know. It may sound awkward, I am going against the tide here by saying something that is not cliche.

But if your data says that the money draining out is more than you can ever recover no matter what maths you apply … still waiting for a miracle to happen would not be something that I would advise.

6. Embrace Technology

Technology has changed the way the world operates. More so, after the pandemic.

The sooner you adopt it for yourself on a personal level as an entrepreneur, the sooner you imbibe it into the culture of your organisation, the faster will be your path to success.

The bottomline here is that this is the age of working smart in addition to working hard.

The logic is simple: if there is a tool that can do a job for you, use the tool instead of doing it yourself. Learn how to run your startup in robot mode.

7. Informed Decision Making

Your startup success depends on the decisions you take as the leader. The decisions you take depend upon what your data tells you. So don't make decisions out of the blue. Let your data tell you what to do. Data is your key to success.

When I say data, it could be your team, your marketing efforts, your customers, your revenue, your expenses, practically every aspect of your business.

The first step towards giving meaning to your data is creating an organised and centralised data store. And then comes having analytic tools which can give you sliced and diced views of the data. For e.g. which Relationship Manager did maximum revenue in this month will involve employee and sales data. Which product appeals more to customers, will involve a study of product and marketing data.

Data and tools to analyse the data will play a very important role in decision making which will decide the path for your Startup

8. Plan frequently

The wise ones say you should spend more time on planning than executing.

And I am a fan of that concept. Sometimes I go overboard though 😊 . "Don't plan too much", said no one ever.

My firm belief is that planning is actually half executing. Half your job is done when you plan. And considering what I mentioned about agility above, planning needs to be done every time you decide to pivot to maintain agility in your business.

Being a fan of tools, I use Asana for all my planning activities, be it personal , professional – for myself and for the teams I work with.

9. Choose your team carefully

Your team is the driving force behind your success.

As the leader, you want to make sure you have a team in place as soon as possible. But mark my words, I am saying this from experience – the time that you would spend on hiring, firing and rehiring is what will be the decisive factor in the growth of your business.

Better still, spend good time interviewing each candidate (yes, make sure you as the founder, CEO, meet each and every person who is hired into the organisation at least for 2 mins if not more).

These are gems who stay till the end, no matter how rocky the boat. And remember gems are never born, they are created and you will play the biggest role in deciding who becomes this gem in your Startup.

10. Listen, Advice, Delegate

This is a tip I will never forget. Being the micromanager that I am, I ended up doing half the work for my team sometimes. And surprisingly even though half their job was done by me, they were never a happy lot. The real good ones want to do the work themselves, make their mistakes, earn their successes, they don't want things to be handed to them on a plate.

The strategy that you should adopt as the leader of your business is to be a good listener to their problems, advice based on your experience and delegate the job as a whole to them with a footnote which says "At the end of the day, it's your call how you do it".

I learnt this the hard way, and that is the reason it is etched on to my mind forever.

11. Never Stop Innovating

Sometimes, I wonder why people make 5 year plans. Well, they do make 5-year plans because investors ask them to.

Considering I recommended planning a short while ago, I shouldn't be saying this really. Make plans all you want, but never stop innovating because it was all etched on to an excel sheet and you don't want to change it . It is an excel sheet for God's sake, it was not carved on stone.

If you ask me, whichever Startups I consult, I see limitless possibilities in the growth of their businesses. Because my mind works full-time on visualising how I could make their products better and in turn make the lives of their customers better.

And believe me when I say, the more you think about what your business can do for your customers, the more ideas will come to your mind giving you boundless vision.

Chapter 5

Which Tech are You?

Which "Tech" are you?

Technology has been touching every aspect of our personal and professional lives. More so after the pandemic since it has forced us to keep the distance by using technology.

Businesses have welcomed technology with open arms, not just during the pandemic but well before it. And because technology became more as a business component rather than an enabler we hear terms like Fintech, Edtech, Medtech and many other such Techs.

You cannot imagine running a business without it and so directly or indirectly , depending on the domain you work in you become one of these techs. Let's understand what each one of them is and where you place yourself.

- Fintech
  - WealthTech
  - InsurTech
- MedTech
- EdTech

- HealthTech

- PropTech

- RetailTech

- CleanTech

- RegTech

- FemTech

- LegalTech

- FoodTech

- BioTech

- MAdTech

- AgriTech

And don't worry.. If you can't find your industry here. Tech has a way of finding a place in every possible industry and bringing an impact to make things easier and faster.

Fintech (Financial Technology)

This domain has been close to my heart since I have spent the last 6 years dedicatedly working on this from scratch. This is where various aspects of Finance are enabled using technology.

This is related to those Startups that seek to transform financial and banking services by applying disruptive ideas by leveraging digital technologies. This term encompasses a broad range of solutions: payment methods of payment, data-based decision making, customer service through chatbots, personalised AI powered services that learn from customer behaviour

Examples : Paytm , Bill Desk, Pine Labs, Incred, Mobikwik, Razorpay, LendingKart, Coverfox

Wealthtech (Wealth Technology)

A subdomain of Fintech. Startups engaging in this activity leverage the latest technologies to enable digital investment and digital wealth management services. One of the segment's most talked-about-proposals are robo-advisors, automated services that use machine learning algorithms to offer investment advisory services to users based on their performance goals, attitude towards risk and other variables such as age and income

Examples : Fintoo, Arthyantra

InsurTech (Insurance Technology)

'Insurtech' is short for technology-led insurance startups. It's a subset of the larger fintech sector, at the intersection of insurance and technology, where companies focus on manufacturing, distributing and aggregating insurance policies

Examples : Acko, Artivati, Mantra Labs, Pentation Analytics, PolicyBazaar, Toffee Insurance

MedTech (Medical Technology)

MedTech includes various products and solutions used to prevent, diagnose, monitor and treat diseases and other health conditions affecting us. Surgical robots, electronic health data systems, PCR testing kits for COVID-19, and digital health trackers — all of these innovations come under the MedTech umbrella.

Examples : Johnson & Johnson, Novartis AG, Abbott Laboratories, Medtronic PLC., Baxter International, Danaher Corporation, General Electric, 3M Company.

EdTech (Education Technology)

EdTech is the combination of IT tools and educational practices aimed at facilitating and enhancing learning. Live to on-demand teaching comes from the rising adoptions of EdTech. Popular examples of EdTech include Massive Online Open Online Courses (MOOCs) on edX and Coursera

Examples : Byju's, Toppr, Awign Enterprises, Classplus , Doubtnut , Masai School , Pesto , Practically , Quizizz

HealthTech (Health Technology)

HealthTech startups are more focused on optimising patient care in general, developing solutions that address a broad range of fields within the health industry: apps for setting up doctor appointments, wearables with sensors to monitor and collect data on the vital signs of patients, apps that help patients prepare for a surgical procedure or video games that help make post-trauma rehabilitation more tolerable.

Examples : Innovaccer, PharmEasy, 1mg, Cure.fit, Practo, Mfine, MediBuddy.

PropTech (Property Technology)

The real estate sector has not been too involved in imbibing technology in its day-to-day activities but with the advent of few incumbents who took PropTech seriously, it has been booming ever since. From the modernization of real estate marketplaces, and blockchain-based home buying and selling solutions, new construction and property management software, virtual and augmented reality technologies to enhance property brokerage services, home automation, IoT devices or the leveraging of big data and geolocation.

Examples : Magicbricks, NoBroker, Infra. Market, NestAway, Livspace, Square Yards, Stanza Living, Furlenco

RetailTech (Retail Technology)

RetailTech has seen a lot of growth during the pandemic because people's desires for shopping were curbed extensively. Bringing online shopping experiences to brick and mortar stores using technologies such as RFID, beacons and virtual reality is one of Retailtech's ultimate goals.

Examples : Aahaa, Bohriali, Ecohoy, Alanic

CleanTech (Clean Environment Technology)

These terms encompass a broad range of tech solutions and business models aimed at minimising the environmental impact of companies. With sustainable development as their guiding principle, these startups focus on everything from resource efficiency, pollution prevention and alternative renewable energies, including sun, wind and biofuel technologies.

Examples : BhuYantra Waste Management, EcoEase,Enfrien Innovations, Enstin Labs

RegTech (Regulatory Technology)

In the post-2008 Global Financial Crisis world, an increase in regulation brought a corresponding increase in regulatory technology. Be it facilitating KYC (Know Your Customer/Know Your Client) requirements, checking for fraud, tracking transactions, managing data, or conducting due diligence — RegTech has helped banks and financial institutions save valuable time and money, and made the regulatory process more robust and easy to comply with at the same time.

Examples : Avantis, Signzy, IDfy, FixNix

FemTech (Female Technology)

Although the term was originally coined in reference to tech startups focusing on the development of female hygiene and health products. Today, it's used to cover a much broader phenomenon that includes other initiatives championed by businesses and associations, which combine feminism and technology to eradicate the gender gap in the technology sector and promote the participation of women in STEM (Science, Technology, Engineering and Mathematics) careers.

Examples : CareMother by CareNx, Sheroes, Smart Scope Cx by Periwinkle Technologies , CervAstra by AIndra

LegalTech (Legal Technology)

Providing technology solutions for core legal processes, LegalTech has become very important for law firms. LegalTech helps with workflow management, document review through artificial intelligence (AI) and machine learning (ML), e-discovery for processing documents, legal chatbots, online lawyer marketplaces and even data security.

Examples : PracticeLeague, LawRato, Presolve360, Legal kart, Ipleaders, Lawyer24x, SoOLEGAL, Legal Salah, and MikeLegal

FoodTech (Food Technology)

This is about the food industry leveraging technology to take a broad range of services to a whole new level: from automated cooks, food delivery, 3D food printers, social media websites to meet new people while sharing a table, restaurants offering virtual or augmented reality experiences, personalised recommendations through virtual assistants, dishes capable of calculating the amount of calories in the servings they hold.

Examples : Zomato, Swiggy, Licious, Faasos, Box8, Magicpin, HungerBox

BioTech (Bio Technology)

Biotech companies strive to develop equipment and solutions that help improve our lives. Some examples of companies include MedLumics, which recently closed a €34.4 million round to launch a device for treating atrial fibrillation in cardiac arrhythmias; Stat-Diagnóstica, which develops technology to detect infectious gastrointestinal, respiratory or meningitis-inducing agents; or Anaconda Biomed, which raised €15 million to build a next generation catheter for the treatment of the acute ischemic stroke.

Examples : Serum Institute Of India, Panacea Biotech Ltd, Biocon Ltd, Novo Nordisk, SIRO Clinpharm, Novozymes South Asia, Shantha Biotech, Indian Immunologicals.

MAdTech (Marketing and Advertising Technology)

Madtech is the application of technology in areas of marketing and advertising through tools that allow to interact with the audience and potential customer base, always to bring an added value that can contribute to boost sales. The term adtech is also used to refer to this type of solution.

Examples : AdzJunction, DigiVigyan, Aristoma, DoYourThing

AgriTech (Agricultural Technology)

The use of technology in agriculture has helped one of the world's most-essential industries become more efficient, productive, profitable and environmentally friendly. Today, AgriTech is helping farmers and agriculturists through smart farming methods such as automated irrigation, hydroponics, scanning and surveillance through drones, better weather forecasting as well as logistics and marketing

Examples : Ninjacart, WayCool, AgroStar, DeHaat, Stellapps, Bijak, CropIn Technology, EM3 AgriServices

So use this as a handy reference to figure out where you belong and I would encourage you to study that domain carefully , keep in touch with the latest happenings. This will also help you identify competitors. Overall study the industry to its core so that you can keep up with its growth

Chapter 6

The 7-Step Startup Success Formula Revealed

Every entrepreneur's journey is a mix of failures and successes. And that is what makes it all worth it.

I packed up all my failures and successes in this box and divided it into 7 compartments which I have fondly labelled as the 7-Step Startup Success Formula.

Your Startup Dream/Idea travels this long enchanting path from an Idea to a Product, and then the Product which goes into the hands of your customer, who, if he/she finds it valuable will eventually even pay for the product.

Let's walk through this enchanting journey as a whole before we delve deep into each step in the upcoming topics. Let's have a feel of what it is to take this Idea from Conceptualisation to a Tangible Business Profit in your bank account.

Step 1 - Developing an Entrepreneurial Mindset

Do you have it in you to become an Entrepreneur? Well, if not, how much are you willing to develop it?

Ultimately no matter how many things I talk about whether it be documentation, whether it be business plan or it may be wireframes, mind maps - the foundational thing that is going to help you take your vision to reality is going to be your mindset as a Startup Founder.

So what you are going to read in this chapter may be a little bit soft skill oriented but these are certain critical characteristics which I observed are completely needed to be a perfect Startup Founder. Having these is going to be the key to success. And this comes from experience. I have been there, done that. Not everyone is born with these skills. Either you have them or you develop them. But there are basic must-have skills which you need mandatorily if you want to be a successful Startup Founder.

Step 2 - Startup Idea Validation using the Idea Validator Framework

The first thing that of course comes through your mind is this Brilliant Idea that you strongly believe will become a huge success. Now ,an idea could come from various sources - maybe it just struck you when you were looking out from your window, staring blankly into space on a relaxed weekend or you heard it from somebody or you read about something similar somewhere and you decided that why not build an enhanced version of it!

It is also possible that you may not have an idea at all. That is also fine as long as you're looking at establishing a business of your own - moving out of the regular run and creating a name for yourself by creating something yourself. When you start off just thinking "I'm done with the regular routine of a daily job where I am reporting to someone, it's high time I venture out to become my own boss." Here's the thing. You can scout for a lot of ideas on the net and see what inspires you, what you can build on and create an empire out of it.

Here's how I started off. I always have many ideas in my mind. Those Saturday mornings when I spend some alone time and look out of my window, staring into space, almost every time (I mean it!) - something new comes to my mind. And I get this strong urge to create a team and start working around it! Well, that is not humanly possible since I can't be starting work on a new Startup every weekend!

So, this is what I do to satisfy my racing mind. I documented all of those ideas.

I have also gone down to the level of breaking them up into sections - The Wishlist is a list of features that the product can have, Expenses gives an indication of what kind of money at a basic level will be needed to set it up, Revenue - the most important aspect - is an indication of how you can make money from this idea.

Which brings us to the next step..Now you may believe very strongly in your idea which is good. Which is a very good positive sign. But do you know whether the idea is saleable or not?

Let me give you a personal example here. I had an idea I was always passionate about - on which I even worked to a certain extent. As a Team Leader, I spent quite a lot of time recruiting software professionals. I did that by visiting regular job sites and hunting for the right person to fit into my team. I did end up finding the right people, but it was quite an effort, I must say. I had to sort through tons of CVs to reach the final candidate. Even though they were found to be so-called "Matches" or they were supposedly coming out of an Intelligent Recommendation Engine, I found that I was rejecting half of them. Maybe my job description was not upto the mark for the recommendation engine to understand what I wanted.

That is where I felt the need - first, for a job portal dedicated to just hard core software professionals so that we could narrow it down. Second, the recommendation engine need not be dependent on the efficiency of the job description. Finding the keywords and throwing out CVs matching those keywords. Maybe I could have the employer upload some perfect CVs and the Recommendation engine should match those CVs using Natural Language Processing techniques. (Sorry, I got a little carried away and sounded technical there 😊)

I embarked on the process to find out whether this idea was saleable or not.I went and did a Google search. Unfortunately I did not find people who were looking for this kind of thing. A search for "job portal for software professionals" revealed irrelevant results. However, that did not set me back. I still had a very strong feeling that this kind of thing is needed in the market because there must be other people like me who are wanting to do this but are struggling. That is when I decided to go out there and ask people. I created an online survey and spread it out to my network as far as I could. And Voila, there were desperate cries by people like me to have something like this which would make their jobs easier.

So there are various ways in which you can find out the scalability for your idea and yes I created a tried and tested framework which I fondly named as the Idea Validator Framework which I will disclose in the topic on Step 2 - Startup Idea Validation using the Idea Validator Framework

Step 3 - Documenting your Startup Value Proposition

Putting down your vision in black and white

So, say you have done your research and the world tells you that your idea is going to be The Next Big Thing. The next step is to document your vision. Documentation is a highly boring activity but having said that it is one of the most integral activities in your entire product development process.

There are two major benefits to documentation. One is when you go out to the world and you want them to believe in your vision it is this very documentation that helps. And secondly more than anything what I experienced on a personal level was that documenting things gives me more clarity and a deeper perspective on my own product. Maybe there are certain things that are there in your mind which are not defined very clearly. But once you start documenting them things become more and more clearer to you. To add to the documentation if there is a proof of concept then you are on another level altogether.

There are many ways to document your vision. There are mind maps, wireframes that you will create. The bottomline here is that there are defined activities you need to do just to give your vision a shape. To make yourself believe in it first and then also make the rest of the world believe that you are up to something really BIG here! We will be discussing all those activities in the topic - Step 3 - Documenting your Startup Value Proposition

Speaking about documentation, the tool that I highly recommend is Evernote. All your text documentation can be neatly arranged in notebooks and notes. You can share it with everyone (even if they don't have Evernote). The concept that made me a biggest fan of

Evernote is that it gives me the ability to write anything anywhere. All my major Eureka moments happen while I'm travelling. At those times, there is an urge to put it down somewhere so that you don't forget once you get off the train. Right there I pull out my mobile from my pocket, open Evernote and jot it down even if there is a crowd of 10 people in a Mumbai local train breathing down my neck at that time.

Step 4 - Product Development (Web/Mobile App)

Time to make the idea tangible

More often than not, I have seen Startup Founders jump right into creating their product before doing groundwork like documentation and Business Plan. Entrepreneurs are an aggressive bunch, they jump into product creation since that is the tangible entity in their Startup vision. This happens because of this strong urge to give their vision a distinct shape.

I have literally had to make many of them hold their horses and prevent them from making this mistake. You have to be very planned and very careful in ensuring that before you create your product your groundwork is in place. The clearer your documentation, your business plan and your vision for the product is - the faster you will be able to bring out the product to the market.

So converting your idea into a tangible product is a step in itself which we will discuss in detail in the topic - Step 4 - Product Development (Website/App) Your product needs to have an online presence. I will be giving you an insight into the aspects of what goes into creating a web version of your product and what goes into creating its mobile counterpart.

Step 5 - Marketing, Sales and Post-Sales

Finally.. Money into your bank account

Last but not the least once you have your product out you have to start talking about it. That is where the branding and marketing and selling comes in.

The internet has a sea of information on various aspects of marketing and selling. There are popularly used terms or jargons related to these aspects. There are even Marketing Gurus who provide their mantras for success.

My experience says there is no single strategy fine grained which is going to work for everyone. Each business has its own charm. It has to be created, nurtured and taken out to the market in its own sweet way. There are strategies and fundamentals which need to be understood theoretically of course. But the real essence is in using those fundamentals in the right way for your Startup Idea to make it work in the way that you want it to.

Step 6 - Identifying the Right Team

Who are they, where do you get them from, what will they do to make your Startup Idea the next BIG thing

Once your vision is documented then you have to think about the team that will actually work to make this vision to become a reality.

My personal opinion here is that you should start small. However it also depends a lot on the vision that you have created for yourself. It is possible that whatever idea you have talked about is such a large scale that you cannot start off with a small team.

Then again there are Startups that have been initiated and taken to a fundamental level at least - by a single person - a Solopreneur - everything right from the documentation to the business plan to the final product development, marketing - Just about everything. Let me reveal a little secret. This person is me! I love to do it this way. However, I'll be quick to add a disclaimer here - it's very hard and gets a little overwhelming at times. So, proceed with caution if you are someone like me. Besides, the Go To Market takes long, scaling the product takes long, so there is a downside to doing it this way.

But if the vision is big enough in terms of scalability, you know that you require an entire team structure in place. The next step is to start thinking about the organisational hierarchy that you want to make your dream happen. This thought process is the most critical one. I'll tell you why.

This happened to me in one of the Startups where I was consulting. The product was ambitious, scalability was high, Go To Market Time came with stringent deadlines. We went a little overboard and created an ideal team structure which would be required if we wanted Go To Market (referred to as GTM from here on) to be 6 months.

Then came the time when we created the Business Plan with the magic numbers to make this happen. Our hearts skipped a beat when we saw the kind of funding that we would need to create this magical team. We had to go back to the drawing board and create a less than ideal team structure, compromise a little on the GTM timelines so that the numbers in the Business Plan didn't jump out of the sheets and give us a heart attack!

And then again, there is that aspect of Should you build in-house or should you outsource. All the pros and cons of both approaches (and yes, there is a third one) which I will discuss in the topic Step 4 - Recruiting the Right Team for your Startup

So, the moral of the story is - decide if you want to build in-house or outsource. If you outsource, you should know how to find the right team. If you build in-house, be very conservative while brainstorming about the "ideal" team numbers and team structure since this is the biggest component of your Business Financials. Proper research on the average salaries for each designation will really help a lot here. indeed.com is the place to go to for these numbers.

Step 7 - Fundraising

Let's rake in the moolah for the Brilliant Startup Idea!

I was never a Finance kind of a person. Technology was always my forte and I just loved sticking to that. Not any more, once I moved on to the Entrepreneurship ride. I tried my level best to pass it to someone else but it didn't work. After all, if it is my Idea, only I know the bits and parts that I need to put together to make it happen. And since I know that as well as the back of my hand, all I need to do is go ahead and research how much each bit and part is going to cost me. And when I say bits and parts - you even have to estimate how much tea you and your employees are going to consume per day. As funny as it may sound, these small costs add on to become significant amounts when you consider a long term vision for your Business. Put them all together and Voila - you have your Business Plan!

Sorry to disappoint you immediately - but let me tell you not so soon. The most difficult but important part is estimating how much money your Business is going to make. When I was told that I will have to do that, I really thought it was a joke. But no. You have to be able to do some market research, check what pricing your competitors have for the similar product and also be able to find out in underhand manners how much they are actually selling.

Now that you have your expenses and your predicted income you come to a Balance Sheet which will clearly give you a picture of your ROI (Return On Investment). This is the most important KPI (Key Performance Indicator) - get used to Business jargon, my friend - to judge the viability of your Business Plan.

So bottomline, whether you are a Finance Professional or not, as a Business owner you have to know how to create a Business Plan. The day you go to an Investor to ask for funding, you will thank yourself for taking this effort because as the Business Owner it gives you a high level of confidence when the Investor knows that you are in control of all aspects of your Business right from the Idea to the final Sale. There is a complete topic on Business Financials creation and I will also provide you with a template so that all you have to do if Fill in the Blanks and your Business Financials will be ready.

Most Startup Founders start off by self funding their vision - Also called as Bootstrapping. In fact there is an entire step by step climb in the funding process which starts from self funding, to family and friends to IPO (Initial Public Offering) where you put up the shares of your Startup in the market out there so that even the General Public can invest in your Startup. We will be looking at all these steps in the topic - Step 5 - Bootstrapping or Fund Raising

Once you have reached the stage where you have to pitch to an Investor, the excitement reaches a high point. It is one of the most challenging milestones in your Startup Journey. How you are going to present yourself to the investors plays a very important role in this entire process of arranging money for your product. The way that you pitch it has to be very defined, crisp and clear because remember that Investors do not have too much time on their hands. Probably you will get a few minutes to present yourself and you want to be sure that you are putting forth the most important points and not beating around the bush just so that you get your message across right and you get the funding that you need from them.

The artefact that you need at this point is a Pitch Deck. We will be looking at the components of a Pitch deck in the same topic - Step 5 - Bootstrapping or Fund Raising

Bringing it all together in a Business Plan

Once you have understood all the 7-Steps and created the documents/artefacts for your Startup, you will put them all in a concise Business Plan which will be your Bible for your Startup.

Having said that, keep it in mind that it will evolve along the way. It is not carved in stone. It may change due to fund availability, market conditions, product evolution, marketing strategies and many other factors.

Be open and be agile when it evolves. And maintain each version so that when you are old and grey you can look back and smile and feel proud to see how you and your business evolved with age and maturity :-)

Ready to begin the Journey?

This entire journey from Idea to Sale is going to go over seven steps. These seven steps have a lot of components in them which I will explain to you step by step. And also I will bring to you on the plate what my real experience was on each of those steps.

So hope you are ready to begin the journey. It is my privilege to hand hold you along the way.

Chapter 7

Step 1 - Developing An Entrepreneurial Mindset

The Entrepreneurial Mindset

Ultimately no matter how many things I talk about whether it be documentation, whether it be business plan or it may be wireframes, mind maps - the foundational thing that is going to help you take your vision to reality is going to be your mindset as a Startup Founder.

Agenda :

- Must-Have Skills
- Gathering the Guts to Quit your job
- How to convert your idea to defined goals

Must-Have Skills

So what you are going to learn in this topic may be a little bit soft skill oriented but these are certain critical characteristics which I observed are completely needed to be a perfect Startup Founder. Having these is going to be the key to success. And this comes from experience. I have been there, done that. Not everyone is born with these skills. Either you have them or you develop them. But there are basic must-have skills which you need mandatorily if you want to be a successful Startup Founder.

A Born Leader

Being a perfect entrepreneur may or may not be possible at the onset. Some of them are born Entrepreneurs and behaving in that manner is second nature for them.

Well, if you don't belong to that category, the good news is this. It is very possible to mould yourself into one. And again, I say this with personal experience. The basic element needed to be an Entrepreneur is to be a Leader. I was not a born leader. I was a reserved person by nature. I hardly even spoke to people, leading them is another ball game altogether. However, I understood during my journey that it is not possible to come into an entrepreneurship role unless you start behaving like a born leader at least.

Even if you are not, you start becoming a people person because it is people whom you are going to interact with. Even as a solopreneur there are going to be clients and vendors you're going to interact with. So to be a leader you have to be a people person and you should know what you want and get it done. Somehow, knowing that you are responsible for getting things done and there is no one else whom you can delegate it to (at least in the beginning) makes you a different person. You change yourself, move out to be an extrovert and get the job done.

Organised and Systematic

The next must-have trait of a Startup Founder is Being Organised. Being organised and systematic is something that I have been literally accused of. I would say accused because being a so-called perfectionist I always ensure that whatever I do is in a completely organised and systematic manner.

And that has actually helped me a lot along the way.

So my suggestion is that maintaining Standard Operating Processes (SOPs as they are popularly called in Business Jargon) - right from day 1 has to be in place. With Startups that I consulted, I made sure they had SOPs for documentation, product development, marketing and even recruitments even though it may not be a direct component of the product creation process. That is half the battle won, the single most important thing.

Emotionally Strong

When someone once mentioned EQ, I gave him a glare. I said it is called IQ, not EQ. He actually glared back and said I meant EQ, I didn't mean IQ. It was embarrassing but enlightening. This person was actually talking about Emotional Quotient (EQ), not Intelligence Quotient (IQ). Another Business Jargon, I said.

Well, I had to eat my words when I actually realised the importance of this aspect of Entrepreneurship. This was not taught to me by anyone, I actually learnt to develop this skill on the job. The entrepreneurship ride is going to be a rollercoaster journey. How high your EQ is is going to determine how you're going to win the race. Being calm at all times is what being an entrepreneur has taught me. So develop this trait if you do not have it otherwise you will not be able to sustain on the rollercoaster ride. Indulge in meditation, do whatever it takes to make you a calm person

Good Negotiator

Being a good negotiator is going to ensure that your purse strings are always tight. That is very important in your capability as an entrepreneur. Sometimes asking for a discount may sound a little bit awkward. But my advice is take the awkwardness in your stride and take the plunge and ask for a discount wherever you can. Remember, every rupee saved is a rupee earned. Every rupee earned is a jump in your ROI which is going to be a very big thumbs up in the long run.

A very good recipe for a perfect negotiation is Barter. If there is a situation where you are not able to afford a service/product, pick up the phone and speak to the provider. See if there is a scope where there could be a barter handshake where you can offer some services to them in exchange for your using their product/service. It has worked like a charm for me in many cases. An excellent negotiation technique which can be used to your advantage if pitched in the right way.

Being flexible

This one is especially very important for those people who quit soft cushion jobs and come on to being entrepreneurs. It is possible that from a lavish office you may move down to a garage or you may start working from home.

You may not have the resources to do everything on the ground level. You have to be ready to roll up your sleeves, get your hands dirty and do everything yourself. Even if it means taking up a broom and cleaning your office because you can't afford the luxuries of a cleaner at the outset. There your flexibility to adjust comes to play. You have to brace yourself for this kind of a change.

These skills are the core foundational skills that you need to have if you are even thinking about entrepreneurship. Entrepreneurship is not a safe and sound joy ride. Like I mentioned earlier, it is a roller coaster ride. If you are adventurous and you enjoy roller coaster rides, well, I'd say - Lucky you! If you are not one of those kinds, sit down in a quiet place and first ask yourself - are you ready to change yourself? I'm not trying to scare you here. All I am doing here is giving you the practicalities and asking you to be prepared for them. If you do not have them attend a course, talk to people, get counselling but develop these skills in you before you jump onto the journey to being an entrepreneur. And if you still don't get them, don't worry. You will develop them along the way.

Gathering the Guts to Quit your job

This is easier said than done. There is a lot of back and forth that goes on in your mind before you decide to break the chains and move on to living a life which is difficult but is more free.

Some tips which can help make it easier :

First of all, ask yourself these questions:

Why do you want to start up? Is it for money, fame, freedom or for solving a problem?

Have you accumulated living expenses for the next 1 year at least?

How much capital do you have? Will you need funding?

Do you have an alternate source of income?

Do you have any liability?

Is there any critical upcoming financial goal in the near future?

Do you possess primary skills to implement your idea?

Do you have a core team or can you hire the best people to implement your idea?

Here's the thing : The answer to all the above questions will never be YES. Some will be NO. But that's ok.

As long as you are 100% committed and confident to achieving what you have set out for, some non-critical ones like will you need funding can be resolved.

The key here is going to be the Idea Validation and MVP (Minimum Viable Product) which you will build in the first 6 months. That will answer most of the doubts that you may have about taking the chance to quit your job and startup.

Even if you take a sabbatical for that much time, in case you are really really apprehensive, I think you should be in a good position, as long as you have accumulated enough for yourself to survive till then.

How to convert your idea to defined goals

When a Startup Founder gets an idea which has a good business potential, he/she doesn't define it as a clear "vision" at the outset. It's just an idea, there are a lot of brainstorming sessions, and then the idea starts taking shape. Slowly and gradually this develops into the Vision.

Idea -> Goals -> Vision -> Features -> Tasks with Milestones.

The first thing that you have to do is to align some goals with your idea. These goals are the strategic objectives of your business. Eventually all your goals aligned together in a single defined statement become your vision. The vision will then be converted into features. Each feature development will involve actionable items or Tasks with milestones.

It is very important to do all these exercises of gradually moving from idea -> Tasks with Milestones. These are the activities which define the foundations for your Startup. These are the keys to your success.

So it is important for you to go to this hierarchy in your head before you actually get down to creating a tangible product.

I will be showing you certain goal cards which will define each goal that is related to your vision.

The links to these gold cards can be found in the description below. I want you to download each of these. I want you to fill in whatever is required in the square brackets for yourself, print it out, laminat it. Keep it in front of you where you can see it everyday because these are going to furnish your mind to really knowing what you want and trying to achieve the same.

Here are the seven gold cards.

The first is my vision goal. My vision is to develop an online product. You can specify your product name and the target audience. You can define it very broadly. So that I can make life easier for them by giving them. For features you can specify the core features or how the product or service that you are offering will change their lives. This is how I defined my vision because when I created this book for you I wanted to make a difference in your life by getting you started off on your Startup Dream.

You're free to put whatever you want but please define this for yourself and have it tangibly in front of your eyes every single day.

The next is your money goal. Let's admit it. We are doing this because it is your passion, your aspiration. But one of the core aims is to make money. You have to define this in numerical values. I aim to make this much money by this date through the sales of this product.

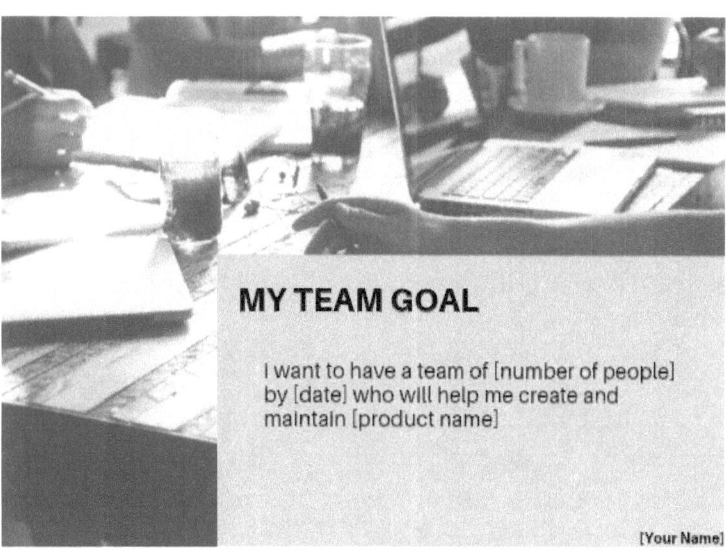

Next comes your team goal.

Like I also said earlier, defining your team is very important. Of course this will evolve along the way but to start off with you have to know who are the must-have team members.

Next is the workplace goal.

I have seen this very often in the minds of people who have visions. The first thing that comes to your mind is what kind of office will I have. Like I said it's okay to start small but nothing stops you from thinking big. Go ahead and put that down on a card and see it every day and I'm sure you'll end up there.

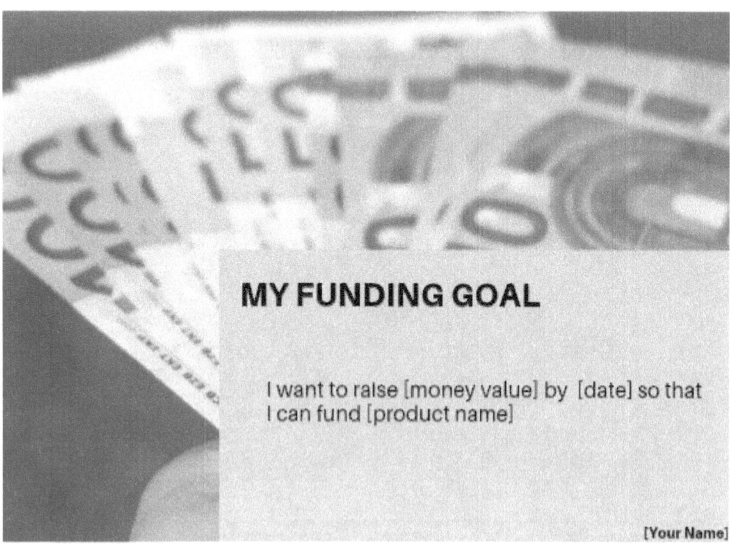

After this comes the monetary aspect of things. At a very high level you should be able to estimate the amount of money that you will need to fund the project. Put it up there and start working towards it.

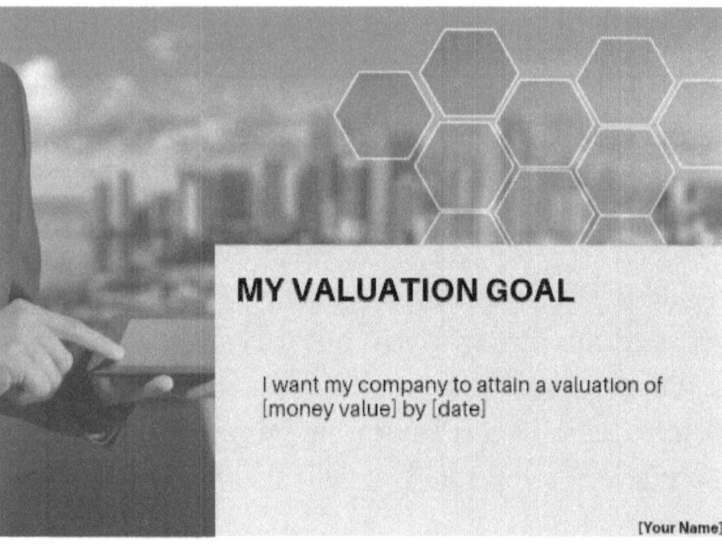

You have to start by setting your aims high. This is not wishful thinking. Your Valuation is what will determine your company's worth in the market. Give yourself a date and create Business Financials which will support you to achieve it.

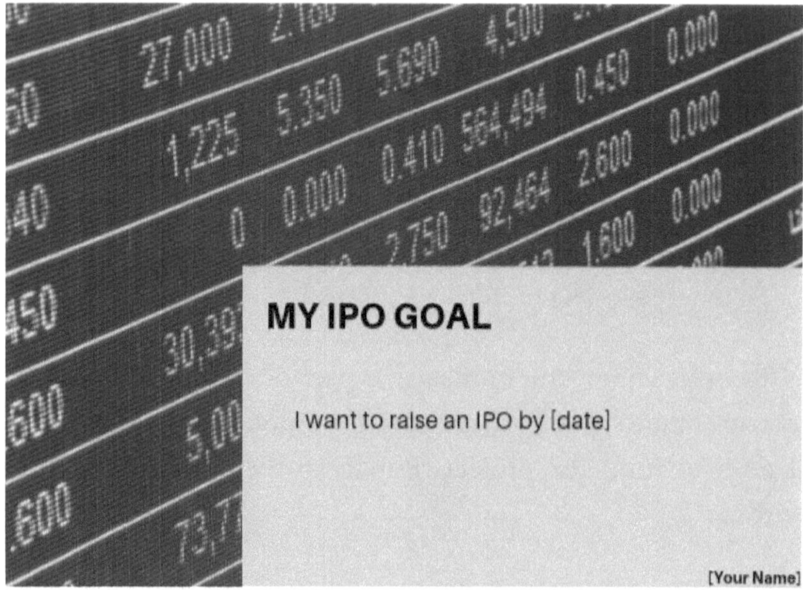

And last but not the least, this will put you in a different bracket altogether. You must have seen so many startups (zomato being the most recent as of date today), filing for IPOs. Set a date for yourself and actually visualise it in your mind where you will find the stocks of your company publicly listed on the NSE.

I would suggest this activity up really really seriously. When I was suggested this activity I was not really sure whether it would make a difference but believe me when I actually went and did that and I laminated it I got it I put it up on my desk the kick was of a different level. So I'm sure you will take this up and you will do this sincerely

And now set your mind at rest, you have already taken the first step by joining this course. Just follow the 7-Step Startup Success Formula to the T and whether you are a born entrepreneur or not you will evolve into one.

So, bottomline, after all it's about the mindset. Just hone your mindset, and success will be yours.

Enjoy the rollercoaster!

Workshop

The purpose of this assignment is to align your vision with defined SMART (Specific, Measurable, Achievable, Realistic, Timely) Goals. There are higher chances that you will make it happen and in the right way at that. So pls make sure you do this however insignificant it may seem

Write, Laminate, Read everyday

http://links.thegreycells.com/VisionGoal

http://links.thegreycells.com/MoneyGoal

http://links.thegreycells.com/TeamGoal

http://links.thegreycells.com/WorkplaceGoal

http://links.thegreycells.com/FundingGoal

http://links.thegreycells.com/IPOGoal

http://links.thegreycells.com/ValuationGoal

Chapter 8

Step 2 - Startup Idea Validation using the Idea Validator Framework

I have seen Startup Founders being super-excited about their ideas and validly so. The most common statement to that effect has been - "This is the next BIG thing!". They have set their minds to this fact. However, if I have played the role of a Mentor in some such setup, I have to be a little strong-hearted and tell them to hold the reins. Not to demotivate them but to teach them to be realistic.

After all, the first litmus test for an Idea to be successful is to find out if it is really marketable and consequently saleable. You need to tweak it around a little bit maybe to suit the market demand. The bottomline is that you have to to really make it work so that those are the initial groundwork activities that absolutely must be done.

Your idea has to ultimately make money. I understand that it is about the vision. It is about the goal , about your dream. But ultimately if your idea does not make money someday those visions, those dreams are not going to be as fulfilling as they should be because ultimately the measure of how successful an idea is or how successful you were in your dream is going to be measured by money in addition to some other factors also. But the prime KPI like I mentioned earlier too is ROI (Return on Investment).

The fame and the recognition that you will get are of course worth the effort. But money is going to be one of the quantifiable measures so you need to know how your idea will finally make money for you to even think about getting into the idea and turning it into a product.

There is a lot of groundwork, a lot of homework that you have to do before you actually get into the implementation of your idea. This is just like when an architect creates a building he/she spends a lot of time on the ground floor level, the base, where you have to establish the core foundations.

There have to be quantifiable reasons why you should be believing in your idea and you are sure that this is going to work.

Agenda :

- Looking for ideas?
- Business Segment
- User Persona/Target Audience
- The Idea Validator Framework
  - Validation before Product Manufacture
  - Survey
  - Competitor Research
  - Google Keyword Planner
  - Google Insights
  - Google Trends
  - Social Proof
  - Pre-Launch Offer

Looking for ideas?

As a Startup Coach/Consultant I must have come across more than 500 Startup Ideas.

There are 2 kinds of Startup Founders. Those who clearly know what they want but don't know how to go about getting it done. And then there are those who carry tons of business experience with them but are still thinking about what Startup Idea could be the next big thing.

For the second category of Startup Founders, I have jotted down my entire collection of Startup Ideas (some which came to me while travelling, some while I was on vacation!).

The goal is to solve pain points for the common man. So, if you always had it in you to launch yourself as an entrepreneur, feel free to pick up any thought and start working on it. If you want me to help you , it would be my utmost privilege.

Business Segment

It is important and not very difficult to classify the segment that your business will be catering to. Sometimes, businesses sell to multiple segments. It is important for you to explore all and decide where your business target segment lies.

D2C Direct to Consumer (D2C)

Brand owners who sell their product directly to their customers without resellers, wholesalers, or distributors. This helps both brand and consumer to conduct a transparent transaction. Example: Glossier.

Social Commerce

A store belongs to an account/individual profile where people can follow, chat with them, engage with them on social actions (like, comment, share, create wish lists, etc) and buy listed products. Facebook and Instagram Stores are a perfect example of this type.

B2C One(Seller) to many(customer)

D2C brands are also considered the B2C models. However B2C business models can sell other brands products as well (Example: A sports store selling Adidas and Nike shoes together)

B2B Many(business) to Many(Business)

WIKI: In B2B there are business people on both sides. B2B has many sellers and different stores. B2B concentrates on raw data for another company. Examples : Udaan, Tradeindia, Alibaba, Indiamart, ExportersIndia.

C2C Many(consumer) to many(Consumer)

In a C2C platform, a buyer can be a seller and a seller can be a buyer. It's an open platform that allows both sides to switch their positions. Example: Fiverr, Etsy, Depop. Classified can also be considered as C2C.

User Persona/Target Audience

Now, take some time and think about this. Would you go out there and shout out from the rooftops to one and all about your product or rather go and talk to the select few with whom your chances of selling the product are much higher?

What is an Ideal Target Customer/User Persona?

Say, you are selling luxury cars. Someone tells you that at a remote location in a rural area huge billboards cost really less. Would you put up a billboard there? Obviously not. Don't take me wrong, I'm not trying to stereotype here, but your chances of selling a luxury car is more if you put up your billboard in an upmarket area where people who have that kind of money reside.

The decision you just took was identifying your **Ideal Target Customer – a person who is very likely to buy your product because of certain characteristics that he/she possesses which make your product very suitable to them.**

Why is identifying your target customer important?

There is a cost that you are paying to acquire each customer – more formally known as the Customer Acquisition Cost.

Marketing Costs are expense guzzlers and must be kept minimal. You might want to check out how you can do that here

The math is simple. When you use Paid Ads on Facebook/Google for example, you pay for each click. You want to make sure the person who clicks is a person who is at least remotely interested in your product, not someone who is casually surfing the net and clicks your ad so that he can kill some time.

That is where spending time on this activity makes sense. Identify your target customer and Paid Marketing channels like FB and Google give you the opportunity to define them in their systems so that they ensure that they market your product only to those who are likely to buy and so that you as the Startup Founder ends up paying minimal cost for the clicks on your ads.

You can find a link to the User Persona Template in the workshops section which will make it easy for you to arrive at that specific person who is likely to buy your product.

Customer Identification Parameters

Complex as it may sound, what this actually means is trying to divide your customers into segments based on some identifying characteristics.

What we are trying to do is group similar characteristics together and try to identify which group is more likely to buy our product.

Here's the thing – We will give each kind of customer a name too. Weird as it may sound, the mention of Peters and Janices or Rahuls and Seemas in a Marketing meet are commonly used to mention a group. These are the User Personas.

A real estate Startup founder discovers based on competitor research that second homes are generally bought by men in the age group 35-45

Geographic Parameters

Postal or ZIP code

City

State

Region

Country

Some examples based on geographic parameters :

A Startup which is in the business of sending Indian goods to people abroad will have parents whose kids are settled abroad as target customers.

A Marathi magazine owner will target people residing primarily in Maharashtra

Psychographic Parameters

Interests

Needs

Preference

Lifestyle

Values

Behaviour

Some examples based on psychographic parameters :

People interested in the Entrepreneur magazine are definitely those who nurture dreams to be Entrepreneurs. These are the ideal customers for a Startup Coach like me.

A Travel app will find it fruitful to advertise to people who have posted pics of themselves at various locations.

User Persona

After having completed the above exercise you would have come up with maybe single, maybe multiple ideal target customers based on your offering.

Say, one set of ideal customers for your Service 1 is in the age group 25-35 with interests such as travel and who earn more than 1L per month. Let's call them the Rahuls. Rahul here is your User Persona for your Ideal Target Customer.

Say, another set of ideal customers for Service 2 is in the age group 60+ with interests in travel and are retired. Let's call them the Rajnaths.

So, next time when you are in a Marketing meet and you want to refer to the 25-35 age group, earning more than 1L instead of describing all their characteristics you would say, "Let's run a campaign for the Rahuls this month".

Here is an explanation of how you can use the template : For now you can ignore the second sheet which contains aspects related to the user journey which we will cover in the Step 4 - Product Development.

https://youtu.be/Vz-G7BLDVgs

The Idea Validator Framework

There are defined activities that you can do to quantify your belief in your idea, to get an idea about what kind of a place your vision has in the market. These are the steps which are going to tell you how saleable your idea is.

Here is the tried and tested Idea Validator Framework which I have developed over the years after a lot of trial and error with Startups that I have consulted and coached.

Validation before Product Creation

Validating the demand for your idea is more important than ANYTHING. More important than the features, your team, the design, the pricing - everything.

Without market validation you'll have a product that you don't know if anyone will pay for. You'll burn a lot of time, energy and money and you'll end up stressed and burned out.

And that hurts - a lot.

OK so let's get to it: here's how to validate your startup idea before you launch, before you invest or raise your very first Rupee, and definitely before you hire anyone.

Identify the Problem, not the Solution

You want to be able to clearly articulate a problem that your target customers experience regularly.

You want to be able to write down your problem in a simple statement. A few examples:

It's impossible to follow up with customers once they have purchased a course.

It's hard to determine which customers will go for an upsell.

I'm a non-technical person. I don't know about websites and apps.

Determine if it is a Tier 1 Problem

It's easy to identify problems—they're everywhere. What you're really looking for is what I call a "tier 1 problem"—which means the problem you're looking to solve is one of the top 3 problems your potential customers are experiencing.

Let's say your (eventual) target buyer is the Founder of a small business. Their top 5 problems might look something like this:

Generate more revenue

Hire a Digital Marketing Manager

Outsource HR

Get better at social media and invest in Facebook ads

If you're planning to sell Digital Marketing as a service, you can see that's NOT a tier 1 (top 3) problem for the typical Founder of a small business—it's #4 on their list.

They'll be so focused on solving their first 3 problems that you'll never get a look in—EVEN if you have the best product, and EVEN if you have the best support. They simply won't have time (or budget) for you if you're not solving a problem that's top of mind for them—a tier 1 problem.

You have identified your target customer above. Make sure he/she is the decision maker where purchase is concerned. Could be the CEO in a small organisation or could be the Finance Head in a large organisation. Basically he/she has to be the decision maker, influencer or approver. Then just connect with all of the prospects you find with a message like this:

Hi [name],

We're hoping to spend 15 minutes on the phone with CEOs who are experiencing [problem]. We're doing research and have nothing to sell. Would you be available for a quick call tomorrow at 3pm?

A few pointers here:

Be short and to the point—don't waste their time.

Include a specific day and time when you want to talk—avoids email ping pong.

Reach out to 3x the number of prospects you actually want to talk to. So if you want to talk to 20, message 60. Most won't reply and some won't be interested.

Great. Now you've got at least 20 people ready to chat who are experiencing the problem you've identified.

Before your first call, you want to come up with the following questions to ask them. The entire outcome of the call is to validate:

Do they experience the problem too?

How painful is this problem for them? (i.e. is it a tier 1 problem?)

How do they solve the problem now? What is missing in that solution?

Would they pay for a solution to the problem if it took care of everything that they were looking for?

Collate the answers from all of your calls in a Google document, Evernote, etc. After 5 or so calls you'll start to get a sense of whether this is actually a big problem or just a "nice to have".

Never, ever build a startup that solves a "nice-to-have-fixed" problem. People will use your product but never pay for it.

Verify There's a Budget for a Solution

If you have existing competitors aiming to solve the same problem, you can look at their traction. Are they growing fast? Do they have a sufficient volume of customers? Are they (or have they) raising money? Are they hiring? Look for clues of growth.

You also want to set a second follow up with at least 10 of the prospects you spoke with on the phone and get their views on pricing.

What we just did was Validation before even creating your product. And the best part? You've spent literally Rs.0 to get to this point.

Marvelous!

Surveys

Surveys are an excellent mechanism to collect information right from the horse's mouth. The participants of your survey have to be similar to the target audience that you have in mind for your product. For example, if my product is a job portal exclusively for the software industry then my target audience is Software Professionals. Conduct a survey directed to this particular subset of people. Ask them how happy it would make them to have such a product on hand. Ask them would XYZ feature excite them. See the responses. If they are good, it will be the best motivator for you. If the responses are not so good, then you can tweak your idea based on the responses to make them good.

There are many free tools out there to help you create a poll/survey. A simple Google search will reveal tons of them. All you have to do is create a Survey, join Facebook/LinkedIn Groups where your target audience is and post the Survey. Interested people will surely revert.

All you have to do is put up a survey out there. Don't say it is a survey to rub it in. Start by something as casual as "Just curious.. ", "Was thinking.. what do you think?". You don't have to disclose to your network that you plan to start something based on the results of the survey. Encourage them to share in their network.

If it really has value, it will spread like wildfire. Well, even if it doesn't, the survey results sample will give you some direction. Make sure the questions are interesting and make people wonder why you are asking them. The questions should make them think rather than be a form which they have to fill which their friend has asked them to.

A very prominent market leader in this segment worth mentioning is Survey Monkey. It started off by providing a tool to create Survey Forms which you could send to your audience and analyse the reports thereafter based on which you could make intelligent decisions. However, over the years SurveyMonkey has added to its Feature Basket aspects like AI Based Market Research. For those who don't know whom to send their surveys too, SurveyMonkey has this feature called Global Integrated Audience using which you can collect quality responses from consumers in minutes with our integrated Audience panel which proudly boasts of 144M+ people across 130+ countries with 50+ profiled attributes and Custom screening. Your survey goes out to this huge audience and the replies that you get will be a sure-shot validation of your Idea.

Keyword Research

At all times you need to be up-to-date with what your competitors are doing.

There is an excellent tool called the Google Keyword Planner which will give you a very clear idea about how much of a demand is there for your vision.

Your vision needs to be converted into keywords. There are some keywords that you already may have in mind. For example if my Startup Visio is to "create a job site dedicated to the software industry", I will probably have some keywords in mind like "jobs for software professionals" or something like that.

There is a clear technique behind this. This is how I do it. I identify Keywords and then I create KeyPhrases based on permutations and combinations of those keywords. For e.g. Keywords could be "JobSite", "Software", "Professionals", "Development" and Key phrases could be "JobSite for Software Professionals" or "JobSite for Software Development Professionals" or "JobSite for Software Developers" and so on. It's all about how deeply you can relate to your vision and think about all possible keywords related to the same.

Once you have these keywords and key phrases, then it is a matter of plugging them into the Google Keyword Planner and Voila! you get tons of other suggestions for your chosen keywords and key phrases. Not only that it also gives you a peek into how many times that keyword was searched in this month or for a previous timeline.

An excellent tool created by Neil Patel (a well known marketing guru) is UberSuggest. This takes you one step ahead and for the keywords and key phrases that you have already identified it gives you an idea about who else is ranking for the same. These, my friend, are your competitors. Keep a watch out for them. Try to create content which can help you rank ahead of them. That's the mission!

On the same lines, SEMRush is another tool which helps tremendously in giving you a sneak peek into your competitor's winning strategies so that you can adopt and improvise upon them to get ahead in the race.

Competitor Research

This has been the most strenuous but most beneficial exercise that I make Startup Founders do when I start coaching them. When I give it out, it looks like a simple Google Sheet which is to be filled. But when they get on to doing it, it requires much more than just filling out the sheet.

Keyword Research will definitely give you a list of most of your competitors. List down parameters on the basis of which you will study your competitors. Their website look and feel, the list of services they provide, whether they have a blog or not, how soon do they revert to a call back request, how much funding did they receive and in which year, what is their employee strength and so on and so forth. When you have that on hand, what you have to do is visit each of their websites/apps and list the details for each parameter.

For some you might even have to call them to snoop and find out what they do. Nothing wrong with that. It is a fair game which all play. Some admit it and some don't.

Once you are done filling up all parameter details for all competitors, it is your turn next. List your values for each of those parameters. This would be an eye-opener. You will realise that you never thought of some things that they do. You will also dance with joy when you realise that there is something that you thought of but they don't have.

It's OK to have feature parity as a baseline, but that should only be 80% of your product. There should be at least 20% that's better—not different just to be different, but distinctly better.

A clear benefit potential customers can see and understand when comparing your product to others. And one that you can position around after you launch.

At the end of the day, it is trying to ensure your Startup Idea is backed up by a vision that beats all in the race or at least stands out. This is where you will come up with your USP (Unique Selling Proposition).

My personal experience has given me one very big insight I have learned from competitors. What you should not do. I looked at the positive things that they were doing. I also looked at the things which were actually bringing them down and I made sure I did not make those mistakes which I regret later.

Google Insights

Google provides a tool for almost everything. The Keyword Planner helps you identify winning keywords. Google Insights - thinkwithgoogle.com gives you a much deeper aspect of any keywords related to your business.

It is like your Personal Research Assistant. Put in a keyword and it will list all possible Articles, Perspectives, Reports and News related to your Business. A thorough study of this will take you miles ahead in terms of developing, nurturing and refining your vision if the need arises.

Google Trends

Google trends will tell you what's hot and what's not.

There are many ways in which you can use Google Trends. Primarily SEO (Search Engine Optimisation) professionals use Google Trends for keyword research so that they can apply techniques to have their websites listed high on Google ranks.

However, I recommend using it to validate one's Startup Idea - mainly because it shows whether people are talking about it. And if they are, you have a winner on your hands!

So, once you have a list of keywords on hand related to your Startup Idea, fire them away on Google Trends and see the magic unravelling in front of your eyes.

You will see how many times over a given period of time those keywords were searched. Not only that, it will also show you related keywords which you probably didn't think about. Make a note of those too since they will help you in SEO (Search Engine Optimisation) of your website in the long run.

An interesting aspect for those whose Startup Idea is related to products which sell seasonally. It also shows you the keyword search spikes over a given season, so you can plan your marketing and inventory on the basis of that.

Apart from variations over time, it will also give you variations over geographical locations. So, when you plan your marketing and sales strategies, you can factor that in. Probably, you had not even thought that your target customer would be in X location, and Google Trends told you so.

When you are just starting off and you need to establish yourself as an expert in whatever field you are targeting, getting an idea about what content is trending on Google trends will help you plan your content marketing strategy. Write content related to trends and see how people respond to it. You will get a good validation of your Startup Idea since people will be quick to respond to it due to its popularity.

A sneaky way to spy on your competitors would be to see where they are ranking for trending keywords and get an idea into their business model to see what works for them and what doesn't. I am not saying you have to copy their business model, but getting an insight into it will definitely let you hone yours so that you can get the edge early on.

The bottomline is that if what you have in mind is trending on Google Trends, then go for it. If not, see what others are doing in the same domain and tweak if necessary to beat the competition and create a winning strategy.

Social Media Proof

Social media is the voice of your customer out there in real time. Make sure you keep your eyes and ears open at all times.

When you are just starting off, you don't even have your product on hand, you don't even know who your customer is, where he/she is out there.. Still, social media can play a very big role in validating your idea.

Here's the thing..

Say, you are all ready with your survey which is going to give you proof of how valid your idea is. Does it have the potential to create an audience and generate money from that audience? Social media is the answer. After all, it all starts at home.

Your own social media account is the point to start. You may find it a little awkward, but believe me when I say you will be overwhelmed by the support you receive from your near and dear ones.

A social media presence of what you have in mind is really going to give a boost to your belief in your idea because the post and the mentions of business ideas like yours on social media are going to give you a bigger confidence in the fact that people are talking about this kind of thing.

You get an edge over the competition because you get to know what people are speaking to them, about them. Basically you'll get the sentiment of the entire market from social media.

Pre-Launch Offer

This is a slight underhand way of achieving our target.

Create a landing page about your product and with an offer. Run paid ads with a basic amount or approach people via Cold Marketing and send them a link to your landing page.

After they fill in information and are ready to buy, show them a page that your product will be launched on XX-XX-XXXX (plan a viable future date) and that you will get in touch with them on that date for the payment.

There are 2 risks here :

- You may end up annoying people

- If your product is not launched on that date, you will have to send follow-ups regarding that.

Workshop

User Persona/Target Customer Identification

The goal of this workshop is for you to identify and define the ideal target customer(s) for your product. Give them a name so that you can create a picture in mind when you think about them from any aspect - be it product development or marketing or Idea Validation.

Use this template :

http://links.thegreycells.com/UserPersona

Validation Before Product Creation

- For your given target customer identify the problems they face which your product could solve.

- Narrow down on the tier 1 problem out of those problems and write a problem statement.

- Create a survey (format given in template). Set your google form to save your survey responses in the same sheet.

  - Template   -   https://links.thegreycells.com/IdeaValidationSurvey

- Look for target customer kind of prospects on LinkedIn.

- Send them a connection request and an appropriate time to call (Connection request message given in the template) or a link to the survey if they don't have the time to talk

  - Message Template - https://links.thegreycells.com/IdeaValidationMsg

- If they come on a call, note down their responses to each of your questions in the same response sheet that you created in the google form response.

  - Template - https://links.thegreycells.com/IdeaValidationResp

Competitor Analysis

The purpose of this workshop is to identify your competitors after thorough research, observe what they do with respect to certain parameters and draw a conclusive analysis.

Identify and mark the nice-to-have and must-have features in different colours and see where you stand w.r.t your competitors.

Identify your top 3-5 competitors.

Visit this link - https://links.thegreycells.com/CompetitorAnalysis

Make a copy and upload it to your Google Drive

Make a list of your competitor names in the columns of the sheet. This is how you do it - Put keywords on Google Search related to your idea. See who else is providing the same product that you intend to provide

Observe what they do for each mentioned parameter and make a note of the same in the sheet

Mark the good things in Green and not-so-good in red. The Green ones are the ones you need to ensure you incorporate in your Vision. Ensure there is at least one such thing which you do that they don't. That is your USP. The Red ones are those you need to ensure you don't do.

Share the link when you are done with the assignment

Keyword Research Using Google Keyword Planner/ Ubersuggest

The goal of this workshop is to identify keywords and key phrases related to your business idea using the tools Google Keyword planner and Ubersuggest. Ubersuggest will also list content ideas related to your keywords which will help you in content marketing to target the same audience.

Here is the template - https://links.thegreycells.com/ KeywordResearch

Market Research Summary Presentation

Summarise all your findings in this PPT Template so that you are ready to present to any stakeholder that you have done your homework to the T!

https://links.thegreycells.com/MarketResearchPPT

Templates

- https://links.thegreycells.com/IdeaValidationMsg
- https://links.thegreycells.com/IdeaValidationSurvey
- https://links.thegreycells.com/IdeaValidationResp
- https://links.thegreycells.com/CompetitorAnalysis
- https://links.thegreycells.com/KeywordResearch
- https://links.thegreycells.com/MarketResearchPPT

Chapter 9

Step 3 - Documenting Your Startup Value Proposition

They say "If you fail to plan, you plan to fail". And very rightly so.

According to me if you haven't spent at least 1-3 months in planning (depending on the size of your vision) you are not ready to start. I have often seen Entrepreneurs jump into product creation. The first thing they do when they have a Startup Idea is create a website. Hold your horses.

Documentation is boring, I agree. But till everything that you have thought in your mind is not in front of you in black and white you will not be able to convert your dream into reality.

Think, plan and then act. That is the right way to go.

Agenda :

- Value Proposition (USP - Unique Selling Proposition)
- Brand Guidelines
- SWOT
- Company Incorporation

Value Proposition (USP - Unique Selling Proposition)

Your value proposition or USP (Unique Selling Proposition) is that feature of your product which distinguishes your product in a beneficial way from those of competitors

When an entrepreneur thinks of a Startup Idea, the first thing that they do is find out if someone else is already doing it. And 9 times out of 10, the idea that you thought was one of a kind and that you were so brilliant to have landed up on it, is already being developed by someone else.

Some entrepreneurs let go of pursuing that idea just because of this reason.

Hello!!! It's ok even if 10 other people are doing the same thing that you thought of doing. Where you can make a mark is by giving the end-user some benefit, some way of solving their problem that their competitor is not doing. It doesn't have to be different just for the heck of it. It has to be better and faster and cheaper.

If you can find that feature in your Startup Idea, my friend you have landed upon the USP for your Startup!

Put it down in a crisp short statement with all keywords highlighted and go conquer the world!

Some examples :

- The Economist - You've seen the news, why not discover the story?
- Tiffany & Co. - The right one is worth waiting for.
- WooCommerce - The most customizable eCommerce platform for building your online business.

- AirBnB - Book unique places to stay and things to do.

- Domino's Pizza - You get fresh, hot pizza delivered to your door in 30 minutes or less or it's free.

- FedEx Corporation - When it absolutely, positively has to be there overnight.

Brand Guidelines

A Brand Guideline is a formal document that defines who you are, what you propose to do, your story, colours that you can be identified with, your logo - basically in various ways it defines your business and establishes an identity for your business.

Whether it is your product or your website or your marketing promotions, there has to be consistency across the various depictions of your brand.

It is important to understand first why you need to define Brand Guidelines formally. Generally the Brand Guideline document is created for sharing with any advertising agencies that you may work with or for that matter for your own in-house marketing team, for press releases etc.

More than that, it is the consistency that it depicts for your business. Let's look at this way. Say there is someone you know who is always prim and proper. Out of the blue one day he walks in with a shabby look. It is going to cause an element of surprise and discomfort when you look at him. :-) . In the same way, your brand needs to maintain consistency. If you decide that your brand's social media voice will always be semi-formal, you can't just host a comedy show out of the blue and break the consistency because people would not relate to your brand then.

There are six given components of a Brand Guideline document. It is not mandatory to define all. Although it is recommended that you do.

- **Brand Story**
- **Colour Palette**
- **Typography**
- **Imagery**
- **Voice**
- **Logo**

Brand Story

Who knew that you would find yourself dazed when someone told you – What's your Startup story? And that too out of the blue!

Something that you have been nurturing in your heart and soul for so long now.. But when someone asked you to elaborate on it, you found yourself tongue tied. Not to worry. Happens to all of us.

Happened to me when I was in front of an investor, all set and ready for a Pitch Meeting. I was all prepared with the most tedious and mind boggling questions like technology used, Artificial Intelligence, Automated Marketing for Lead Generation and blah blah blah.

And then, when all he said was – "Anu, tell me your story", I went pale. All I said was a bunch of words filled in with a lot of "You know.. You know.." which meant I was buying time to think what to say!

After that lesson, well learned, next time I went prepared more from the heart, than from the mind and here are a few points from my learning..

1. Focus on the Customer's Pain Point

It all begins with a Problem.

A genuine problem someone faced which you decided you would solve for them. It could be close to home, in your personal network. It could be something you saw on the road. The trigger could be anything. Anything that needed solving – and you jumped in like a Knight in Shining Armour to resolve it.

Leah Neaderthal saw friends struggling with Sales. That inspired her to start her business Growthworks Solutions

Peter Boyd, a lawyer, began PaperStreet Web Design, because he could not take the fact that Law Firms had awful websites.

Daisy Jing of Banish had an acne problem! She decided she would help people by addressing them on YouTube. It was these people that inspired her to create her own line of products.

Think about what was the story behind the problem that inspired you to start up and pen it down with all your heart and soul. Put yourself in the shoes of the person facing the problem and describe it with the same pain that they would have felt dealing with it.

2. Propose how you plan to solve the Customer's Pain Point

Solutions and advice are plenty and freely available when a problem is presented.

The idea is to have a clear action plan after a deep assessment of the problem at hand. Not just an action plan but an action plan with timelines and milestones. That is a real solution!

It gives the person facing the problem a hope of a tangible solution. Without that your solution story is incomplete. Evaluate and brainstorm from all aspects to cover any loopholes that may creep up.

Think and propose as to how you plan to reach out to others who are facing the similar problem. You need to have a clear strategy as to how you are going to shout out from the rooftops to all the relevant people that you have a solution to their problem.

Yes, I am talking about How you plan to market your product.

Colour Palette

This one is interesting! Wish I knew it when I chose my brand colours. This is embarrassing but I have to admit I selected my brand colours - grey and orange, because I really liked the combination

Now I know there is a complete theory behind colour psychology. Here goes.. Some explanations related to colours and some brand examples for each.

Red

Red colour triggers powerful positive and negative emotions, urgency, adrenalin - sets the pulse racing.

Image ref : Hubspot

Orange

Generates a feeling of warmth - bright, light and fun

Image ref : Hubspot

Yellow

Yellow represents sunshine, youthfulness, brightness (like orange)

Image ref : Hubspot

Green

Green is synonymous with agriculture, health, environment.

Image ref : Hubspot

Blue

Blue represents cool, calm, strength , wisdom and is generally categorised as a corporate colour.

Image ref : Hubspot

Purple

Purple is related to superiority or royalty and prestige. Also has a feminine touch to it due to is closeness to pink.

Image ref : Hubspot

Magenta

Magenta, being dark pink is closely related to femininity and often youthfulness.

Image ref : Hubspot

Black

Black donotes luxury and power. Interestingly most unicorns have black, white or grey as their brand colours.

Image ref : Hubspot

White

White clearly represents clean and neat.

Image ref : Hubspot

Typography

Typography is the selection of fonts to be used across your logo, website, product and marketing promotions.

I am not saying you have to use only those all across mandatorily, but it is recommended to maintain the consistency of the brand.

Here is a helpful guide based on what you brand is supposed to project :

Here are the personality traits of the 6 top font categories:

- Serif fonts are classic, traditional, and trustworthy

- Sans-serif fonts are modern, clean, and help create minimal designs

- Slab serif fonts are bold, quirky, and confident

- Script fonts are elegant and unique

- Handwritten fonts are informal and artistic

- Decorative fonts are stylized, distinctive, and dramatic

Imagery

Of course you will use different images as the need demands - be it the website, product images or marketing promotions. But defining the basic imagery for your brand helps to ensure you are not going off track or conveying a wrong message.

Generally what is recommended is a Mood Board.

Mood board: Collect images that convey the feeling that you want people to get when they interact with your brand.

Voice

Brand voice is the tone of your brand. It strongly affects how your audience feels about you.

Use the following tips to define what your brand voice is.

- Build on personality: Remember that list of 3-5 adjectives that describe your brand personality? Use that to describe the type of language that is on-brand. Example - If you are a brand representing youth, it's ok to use slang in your marketing promotions, not so if you target a corporate audience.

- Do's and don'ts: Pick words you like and words you don't to clearly demonstrate what your brand voice is. E.g. you don't want your brand to use jargon in its content marketing. You want to keep it simple so that a layman can relate to it.

Logo

Your logo is the most distinguishing factor about your business. Make sure you spend good time on it before deciding to freeze it since you would never want to revisit it to change it.

Having said that, there are many popular brands like Apple which have changed their logo over time. As a personal suggestion, I don't recommend it.

There are simple logical points to keep in mind while finalising your logo

- The logo should have the selected brand colours

- It should have images which are consistent with the selected imagery for the brand.

- Consider the spacing that you want around it carefully for the image to be legible.

- The tag line must focus on the USP and must be short and concise and eye-catching.

- Your logo should be unique. Don't copy.

- It should represent the voice of your business. An agriculture logo with money as its image will convey the wrong message.

- Ensure your graphic designer gives you various resolutions and various formats (eps, png, jpg) of your logo for print, web etc. (www.fiverr.com is a good place to get your logo done). Make sure you get the original file of the logo from them and keep it safe.

SWOT Analysis

SWOT stands for Strengths, Weaknesses, Opportunities and Threats.

As an entrepreneur you are in high spirits. You are absolutely confident about your business. Nothing wrong with that. But once in a while, it is advisable to play the devil's advocate and even look at it objectively from a holistic point of view.

Hence this activity of SWOT analysis which will give you a holistic view of your Startup from all angles and give you the opportunity to take appropriate action.

STRENGTHS	WEAKNESSES
What features of your business are you proud of?	What could you improve about your business - be it processes, product features, marketing?
What unique assets can give you an advantage?	Where do you have fewer resources than others?
What did the competitor analysis tell you about what you were doing better?	What did the competitor analysis tell you about where you were lagging?
Is your team good?	Does your team have gaps that need to be filled?
Do you have requisite funding?	Do you have requisite funds?
Does your business have good technology backing?	Is your business traditional or legacy that does not use technology as a backbone?

OPPORTUNITIES	THREATS
Does your market research indicate any opportunities that can give you the desired boost? Are there any current market trends could you take advantage of? Are there any regulations that may impact your company positively? How can you turn your strengths into opportunities?	What threats could harm your business? What is your competition doing that could be of danger to your business? Are there any current market trends that could affect your business? Are there any regulations that may impact your company negatively? What threats do your weaknesses expose you to? Could there be too many competitors to make it a red ocean market in the future?

You can access this template here - https://links.thegreycells.com/SWOTAnalysis

Make sure you have given each answer as objectively as possible. Quantify where appropriate to give clarity.

How to use the SWOT Analysis

Make an ACTION PLAN with DEFINED TASKS AND MILESTONES for the each of the following

- Can your strengths open up new opportunities?

- Can your strengths mitigate some threats?

- Address each weakness one by one and crush it to the core.

- Grab each opportunity and see how it can be applied to boost revenue and profitability.

- Address each threat and create a separate back-up/mitigation plan for each.

- Prioritise tasks and delegate as appropriate.

SWOT Analysis Example

Consider a hypothetical Fast Food Joint MacBurger, planning to set up stores in all Tier 1 Cities in India, starting with Mumbai. Their CEO decides to conduct a SWOT Analysis in a brainstorming session with the CTO and CMO.

STRENGTHS	WEAKNESSES
Uniqueness : MacBurger will serve unique burgers with fillings which are not run-of-the-mill. **Location** : Tier 1 cities will have the buying potential to eat out frequently. Also, the young population would prefer fast food. **Food Choice** : Burgers are the most popular fast foods and we specialise only in Burgers - various types	**Funds** : Setting up stores would require a lot of upfront funds. **Franchise Scouting** : Will have to search and identify potential business owners who can set up franchises in various cities. **New Entrant** : New chain will take time to establish itself.

Technology Backbone : We have a strong technology team	
OPPORTUNITIES	THREATS
Tech Savvy population : Will be receptive to online ordering and can be influenced by Digital Marketing **Tier 1 City Growth** : New residences and offices keep coming up. We can use the first mover advantage at many such locations and set up shop there before anyone else does.	**Competition** : Too many fast food joints of other kinds **Product Saturation** : Just burgers could become saturating after a point if we don't maintain the variety

Company Incorporation

Company incorporation and associated legalities are a separate project in themselves. From one entrepreneur to another my suggestion would be to avoid the unnecessary hassle of trying to understand it yourself. Hire an expert, they will ask you the right questions, give you the suggestions, ask you for documentation and complete the formalities themselves.

Some aspects to consider from this point of view :

- Company Registration
    - Proprietorship/Partnership/LLP/Public/Private/NGO
    - GST Registration
    - PAN/TAN Registration
    - MSME Registration

- Startup India Registration
- Legal Protection
  - Trademark Registration
  - Copyright Registration
  - NDA (Non-Disclosure Agreement)
  - Equity Documents
  - ESOP Agreements
- Compliance
  - Corporate Return Filing
  - Appointment of Director (DIN)

  Some experts in this domain :

- https://www.legalwiz.com/
- https://www.startupwala.com/
- https://www.indiafilings.com/

Workshop

USP

Identify one unique aspect of your product/service which solves a critical problem for your target customer in a faster/cheaper/in any way better way than your competitor.

Put it down in one single line. [Include it as a tagline when your logo is ready]

Brand Guideline Document

Create a Brand Guideline document using this template -https://links.thegreycells.com/BrandGuidelines

SWOT ANALYSIS

Gather some colleagues or friends/family and setup a brainstorming session to perform the SWOT analysis of your business.

Use this template - https://links.thegreycells.com/SWOTAnalysis

Templates

- https://links.thegreycells.com/BrandGuidelines
- https://links.thegreycells.com/SWOTAnalysis

Chapter 10

Step 4 - Product Development (Web/Mobile App)

Technology is not a nice-to-have component of any business these days. It is a must-have. More so after the pandemic.

The best way to reach out to the universe is through the internet, and if you don't have a presence there, you stand to lose out even if you are reaching out to the person next door.

Just creating a web/mobile app for the heck of it without planning causes more harm than good. There is a defined strategy in terms of user experience to ensure that you meet your end goal w.r.t product sales, be it a direct online sale or an enquiry or a call to connect your prospective customer to you.

Agenda :

- Habit Forming Perspective
- Mind Map
- MVP
- Paper Prototype
- Wireframe
- User Interface

- User Experience/Journey

- App Development

- Common Modules

- Artificial Intelligence

- Data Privacy

Habit Forming Perspective

[Ref : Hooked - By Nir Eyal]

This is about understanding your target customer habits deeply so that using your product also becomes a habit for them.

I will be explaining this on the basis of an example related to an online investment app. I have tried to understand each habit of my target customer and relate my app development to it so that whenever the user thinks of investment they should open up my app.

This analysis is done from 5 perspectives :

- Habit Zone

- Triggers

- Action

- Variable Reward

- Investment

The Habit Zone

- What habits does your business model require?

  - Regular investment habit.

  - Periodic checking of investments being on the right track

- What problem are users turning to your product to solve ?
  - All investments at one place - doing and checking
- How do users currently solve that problem and why does it need a solution ?
  - Investments are done at AMC websites in case of MF, banks for loans, government schemes
  - Checking of investments is also at disparate places where investment is done
  - Coagulation of all is to be done by the user himself
- How frequently do you expect users to engage with your product?
  - Weekly (to check investments)
  - Need case based - to make investments
- What user behaviour do you want to make into a habit ?
  - Tracking investments

Triggers

- Who is your product's user?
  - Age : 25-65
  - Gender : Male/Female
  - Concern : Wants to have a one-stop place to make and check investments
- What is the user doing right before your intended habit?
  - Has finished work and settled down peacefully and starts thinking about investments
  - Got up fresh on a weekend morning and feels this is a good time to make or check investments

- Come up three internal triggers that could cue your user to action. [Refer to the 5 Whys method]

  - User wants to invest

    - Why does the user want to invest

    - To grow his money

    - Why does he want to grow his money

    - To meet his financial goals

  - User wants to check his investments

    - Why does the user want to check his investments

    - To know if they are giving him positive returns

- Which internal trigger does your user experience most frequently?

  - Need to check investments

- Finish this brief narrative using the most frequent internal trigger and the habit that you are designing : "Every time the user (internal trigger), he/she (first action of the intended habit)"

  - Every time the user wants to track his investments he logs into a tool like Fintoo to check his investments

- Refer back to the question about what the user is doing right before the first action of the habit. What might be the places and times to send an external trigger?

  - Late evening on email/sms/app notification/ad while browsing social media/viral video/referral email/sms/

  - Weekend morning on email/sms/app notification/ad while browsing social media/viral video/referral email/ sms

- How can you couple an external trigger as closely as possible to when the user's internal trigger fires?
  - Internal Trigger
    - Check investment
    - Make investment
  - External Triggers
    - Types
      - Recommended funds
      - Periodic portfolio report
      - Auto rebalance notification (if subscribed)
    - Modes
      - Email (Paid)
      - SMS (Paid)
      - App notification (Paid)
      - Ad while browsing social media (Paid)
      - Weekend blog summary (Owned)
      - Viral Video (Earned)
      - Referral Email/SMS - Coax someone to pass educative info about an investment doing well, since people tend to listen to their peers/relative about money(Relationship)
- Think of at least 3 conventional ways to trigger your user with current technology (emails, notifications, text messages, etc) Then stretch yourself to come up with at least 3 crazy or currently impossible ideas for ways to trigger your user (wearable computers, biometric sensors, carrier pigeons etc) You could find

that your crazy ideas spur some new approaches that may not be so nutty after all. In a few years new technologies will create all sorts of currently unimaginable triggering opportunities.

- Investment game
- Personalised Postcard sent on address- "Congratulations. These investments of yours have performed really well"
- Portfolio bytes on wearable
- Monthly personalised portfolio update book

Action

- Walk through the path your users would take to use your product or service, beginning from the time they feel their internal trigger to th epoint where they receive their expected outcome. How many steps does it take before users obtain the reward they came for? How does this process compare with the simplicity of some of the examples described. How does it compare with competing products and services
  - User wants to make an investment
    - Registers/Logs into Fintoo
    - Checks investments instruments
    - Adds to cart
    - Pays online to make investment
  - User wants to check investment
    - Registers/Logs into Fintoo
    - Checks and analyses portfolio dashboard
    - Delves more inside to check details

- Which resources are limiting your users' ability to accomplish the tasks that will become habits?
  - Time
  - Brain cycles (Too confusing)
  - Money
  - Social deviance (outside the norm)
  - Physical effort
  - Non-routine (too new)
- Brainstorm 3 testable ways to make intended tasks easier to complete
  - Email/App/SMS notifications for portfolio status
  - Recommended fund notifications (app/email/sms)
  - Periodic detailed reports
  - Market bull and bear phases and related investment strategy
- Consider how you might apply heuristics to make habit-forming actions more likely
  - Motivation
    - Keep them motivated to ensure investments are on right track. Instil fear of wrong investments remaining wrong for a long time
  - Ability
    - Reminders
    - Customised dashboard
    - Clear CTAs on external triggers
  - Triggers
    - Listed above

Variable Reward

- Speak with five of your customers in an open ended interview to identify what they find enjoyable or encouraging about using your product. Are there any moments of delight or surprise? Is there anything they find particularly satisfying about using the product?

  - All investments at one place!

  - Online investing for all types of instruments

  - Awesome Portfolio analysis

  - Auto portfolio rebalancing

- Review the steps your customer takes to use your product or service habitually. What outcome (reward) alleviates the user's pain? Is the reward fulfilling, yet leaves the user wanting for more?

  - Mentioned above

- Brainstorm 3 ways your product might heighten users' search for variable rewards using :

  - rewards of the tribe - gratification from others

    - App congratulations notification if an investment is doing really well

  - rewards of the hunt - material goods, money or information

    - Money growth with positive returns

    - Recommendation of funds

  - rewards of the self - mastery, completion, competency or consistency

    - Achievement of investment goals

    - Convenience of investment

Investment

- Review your flow. What "bit of work" are your users doing to increase their likelihood of returning
  - Logging into the app regularly to check investments
  - Setting auto deduction for some investments
  - Subscribing to reminders
  - Spending time on portfolio
  - Applying recommendations
- Brainstorm 3 ways to add small investments into your product to :
  - Load the next trigger
    - General next triggers at all places
      - Subscribe to emails/sms
      - Visit blog
      - App notifications
      - Follow on social media
    - Makes investment
      - Cross sell other investment instruments
      - Check out minty for holistic advice
    - Checks portfolio
      - Show next reminder to review
      - provide an option to setup an ad hoc review
      - Suggest auto portfolio rebalancing
  - Store value as data , content, followers, reputation and skill
    - Data

- - Link bank accounts
  - ITR data
  - Investments performance
- Content
  - Money education (Blogs, Emails, weekly digest)
- Followers
  - Social media
- Reputation
  - Client testimonials
  - Referrals
- Identify how long it takes for a "loaded trigger" to re-engage your users. How can you reduce delay to shorten time spent cycling through the hook?
  - Mostly a minute - Email, SMS, App notification etc

Habit Testing

(TO BE ANSWERED AFTER PRODUCT LAUNCH AND DOING COHORT TO ANALYSE USERS AND THEIR BEHAVIOURS AND THE TWEAKS NEEDED TO IMPROVE THINGS)

- Perform habit testing as described to identify the steps users take toward long term engagement
- Be aware of your behaviours and emotions for the next week as you use everyday products. Ask yourself
  - What triggered me to use these products? Was I prompted externally or through internal means
  - Am I using these products as intended?

- How might these products improve their onboarding funnels, reengage users through additional external triggers, or encourage users to invest in their services?

- Speak with 3 people outside your social circle to discover which apps occupy the first screen on their mobile devices. Ask them to use these apps as they normally would and see if you uncover any unnecessary or nascent behaviours

- Brainstorm 5 new interfaces that could introduce opportunities or threats to your business.

Mind Map

Mind-Maps are a visual representation of your thoughts in the form of circles and lines connecting them. It starts with a central thought. Then you break up the central thought into further thoughts and branch them out from the central thought. You keep doing it till you reach the final fine-grained thought that you can reach.

You can create mind-maps using tools like www.justinmind. com

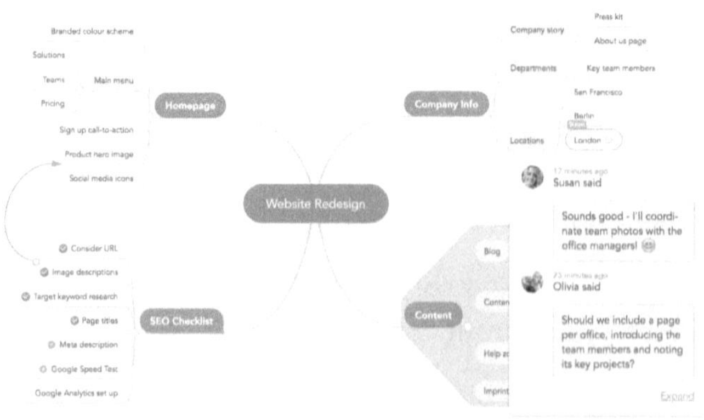

Image Ref : https://www.mindmeister.com/brainstorming

Minimum Viable Product (MVP)

As a Startup Founder your enthusiasm is at its peak. And understandably so. You want to do everything that can boost the chances of your Startup reaching heights. Every new day brings a new idea into your mind. And along with it comes the urge to run to your development team and tell them to incorporate it ASAP.

Somewhere, you need to apply the brakes.

It is fine to list every new feature that comes to your mind. I often find myself noting down the best idea in Evernote while I'm travelling. But it is in your interest to weigh its relevance to the Minimum Viable Product (hereafter referred to as MVP) and then walk upto to your development team and ask them how they can fit it in.

What is this MVP anyway?

MVP is a term which originated in the Lean Startup concept created by Eric Ries.

In simple terms if we understand the 3 words that it is constituted of, it means, the Minimalist version of the Product that represents your Startup Idea which is Viable to satisfy the core pain point of your customers in a satisfactory way.

In more simpler terms, just create that version of your product that is enough to represent your Startup Idea and reduces your Go-To-Market time. The smaller your Go-To-Market time, the faster you get validation for your Startup.

How does MVP make your product development Agile?

Agile is another buzz word you hear in relation to product development.

Being agile in the real sense of the word, means being quick.

And when we talk about agility in Product Development, what it means is delivering quick small versions of your product (which make sense), testing them and then thinking what should be the next feature that should be lined up in the product backlog.

So, if you focus on building the MVP first you are actually following agile principles since you are creating a bare minimum version of your product and then leaving the rest of the features to come up in iterations.

Pain-Feature-Gain

When you talk about Product Development, Steve Jobs plays on your mind. And so rightfully he said **"You've got to start with the customer experience and work back towards the technology – Not the other way around"**

Your MVP is not going to strike you as a sudden realisation out-of-the-blue. It has to be planned on the basis of the customers and their experience related to your product.

It has to start with you working out a Mind Map of all the entities in your Product Ecosystem. It involves the customer, it involves you as the admin, maybe your support staff and so on and so forth. Basically, it involves identifying each entity that will interact with your product.

Focus on the customer now. And see, what are the various ways in which he/she would interact with your product. A very good strategy to do this is the Pain-Feature-Gain method.

For example, a Pain point for a customer would be to talk to an expert. The Feature that you could provide to satisfy the customer is Book an Appointment. The Gain for the customer would be that they are able to talk to an expert.

Now follow this step-by-step process and your MVP will be in front of you in no time.

List out all such Pain-Feature-Gain combos that come to your mind.

Once that is done, write Must-Have/Nice-to-Have beside each of them.

Take the Must-Haves on top in Version 1 of your Product Release.

Take the Nice-to-Haves in the later versions.

There! Your Version 1 release is your MVP.

A note of caution here. Stop the urge to mark everything as Must-Have!

Product Release Estimation

Software Developers are a cursed lot. When nothing else works, curse the software developer for not creating the product well and creating it on time.

I was one, so I know what pain we go through!

There has to be a calculated approach to deciding how much time the MVP (or for that matter even future releases) are going to take.

If the product backlog is clear there is definitely a mathematical approach to deciding how much approximate time it will take to complete the backlog.

The elements of product development to be considered in order to estimate timelines :

Pre-Development : Product Architecture, Epics, User Stories. These are nothing else but your Feature list broken up into actionable elements. The longer that the developers spend time on this, the better will the estimation be

UI/UX : There are 2 aspects that developers consider here. Look and Feel and Navigability. This is not a compulsory pre-requisite to Business Logic Development mentioned below. But if this can be done before hand, it gives much more clarity to the pipeline

Business Logic Development : This is the heart of the development which is undertaken by the core Software Development Team. It could be you if you are a developer and decide to develop it yourself or it could be someone you have hired to outsource your project to.

Coding and Unit Testing : The actual time taken by the developers to write the code and test it from their side.

Unit, System and Integration Testing : This is the evaluation of correctness of each feature developed. After this is done, some time is given to the development to correct any issues and suggestions that come up.

Product Owner Testing : This is the evaluation of correctness done by the Product Owner. And here's the catch in this case. At this stage, all small bugs are expected to be solved, the app is just tested for functionality correctness. After this is done, some time is given again to the development to correct any issues and suggestions that come up.

If you are a non-technical founder, this may seem a little technical in nature. You are not supposed to know the core technology aspects of software development. But you need to know the phases so that you can understand the estimations given and arrive at a common ground.

The final aim is to ensure your MVP and all the future versions of the product are released in time so that your Go-To-Market is reduced and you can get quick validation of your Startup Idea.

MVP Example

Adam's Startup Idea is an Interior Design App.

He has identified his Target Customer as Sophie who is a 30 year old working woman. She has decided to revamp the interior design of her house.

Adam contacts Sophie and this is what she says are her pain points :

There is so much to address w.r.t all the rooms of her home, that she is not able to organise things and it is becoming overwhelming.

She has got multiple quotations from vendors and she does not know whom to choose

If she could visualise the design before she gives a go-ahead it would be great.

Adam lists the above requirements in a Pain-Feature-Gain format

PAIN	FEATURE	GAIN	MUST-HAVE / NICE-TO-HAVE
Overwhelming	Organising elements of work by room e.g. set up a lounger in the dining area Organising elements of work by category of work e.g. civil, electric, carpentry etc	Systematically identify and tackle	Must-Have
Multiple Quotations	Compare Quotations	Neat comparison table with each element compared to pick the best one	Must-Have
Be able to see before deciding	Visualise Design	Can take an informed call after design is presented in a tangible format	Nice-To-Have

Once this is done, Adam clearly knows that the first 2 features are such that the product would not make any sense, till they are done. His MVP is right there.

Adam now goes to his development team who estimates Pre-Development, UI/UX, Business Logic and Testing timelines and comes up with a clear date as to when he can plan his Launch.

You can find the template here - https://links.thegreycells.com/ProductPlan

https://youtu.be/fveM3iSjbvM

Paper Prototype

FRONT END

Get professional resume
Get trained to get an edge
TESTIMONIALS
1
2
3
MORE
Post your resume
Test your aptitude & knowledge.
Home About Services Employers Jobseekers Contact
@ Copyright Web grizzly

Plans & Pricing
EMPLOYERS — JOB POST PLANS
FREE
1 JOB POST
2 JOB POSTS
10 JOB POSTS
MONTHLY
GO FOR IT
PURCHASE
EMPLOYERS — RESUME DATABASE ACCESS
FREE
50 DOWNLOADS
100 DOWNLOADS
GO FOR IT

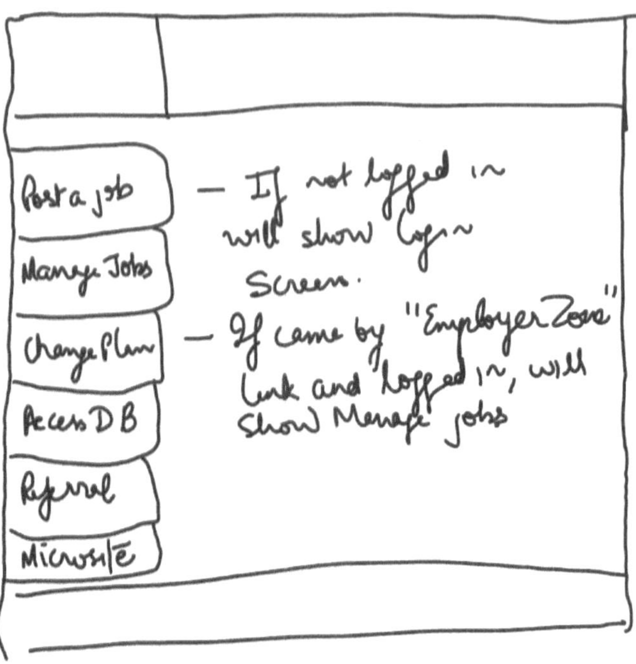

Post a job
Manage Jobs
Change Plan
Access DB
Referral
Microsite
— If not logged in will show Login Screen.
— If came by "Employer Zone" link and logged in, will show Manage jobs

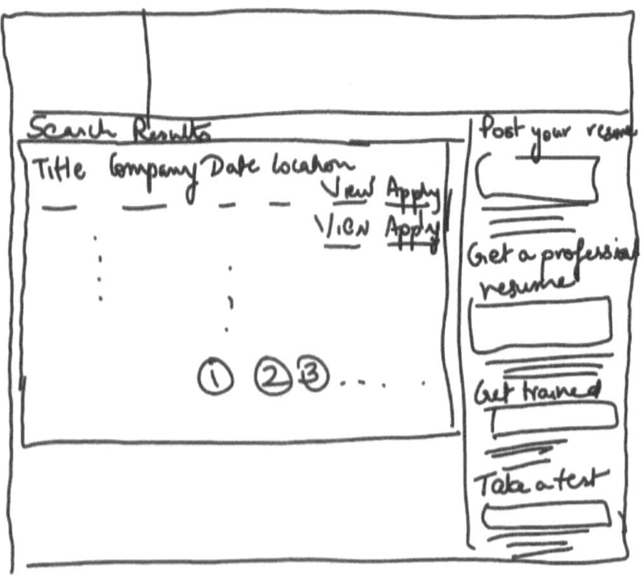

Search Results
Title Company Date Location
View Apply
View Apply
1 2 3 . . .
Post your resume
Get a professional resume
Get trained
Take a test

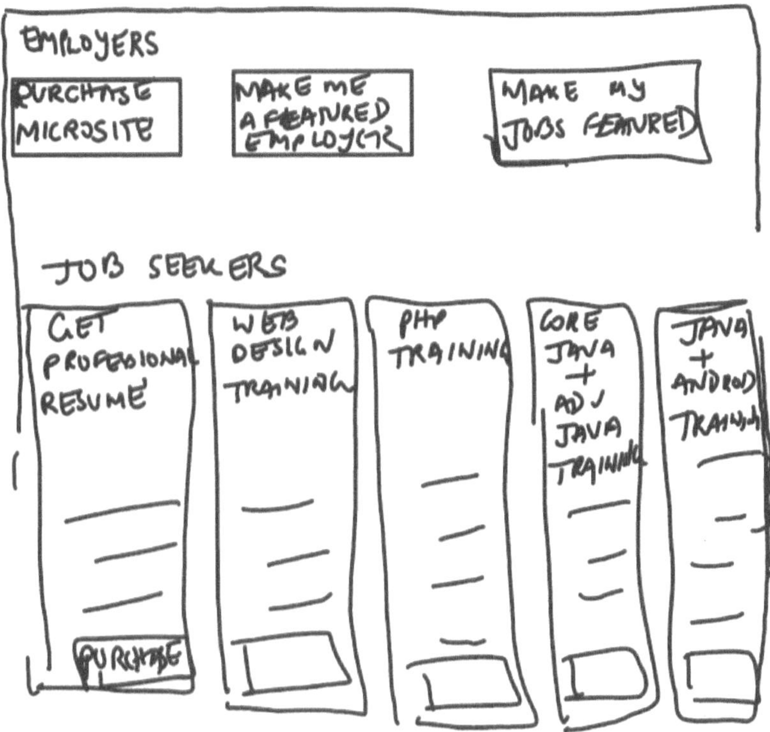

Wireframe

A wireframe is a schematic, a blueprint, useful to help you and your programmers and designers think and communicate about the structure of your website/app

You can create wireframes like the following for each page, based on your paper prototype using tools like www.moqups.com or www.figma.com

Some Example Wireframes

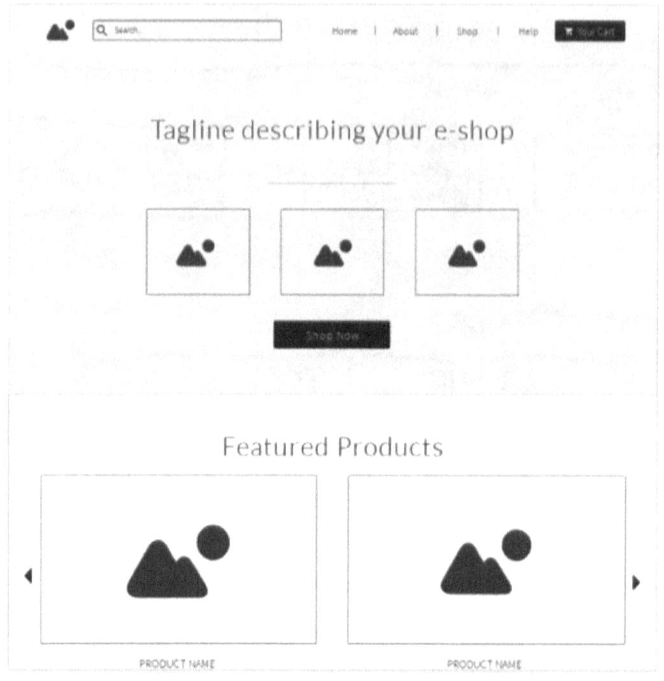

Search
Home | About | Shop | Help
Your Cart
Tagline describing your e-shop
Shop Now
Featured Products
PRODUCT NAME
PRODUCT NAME

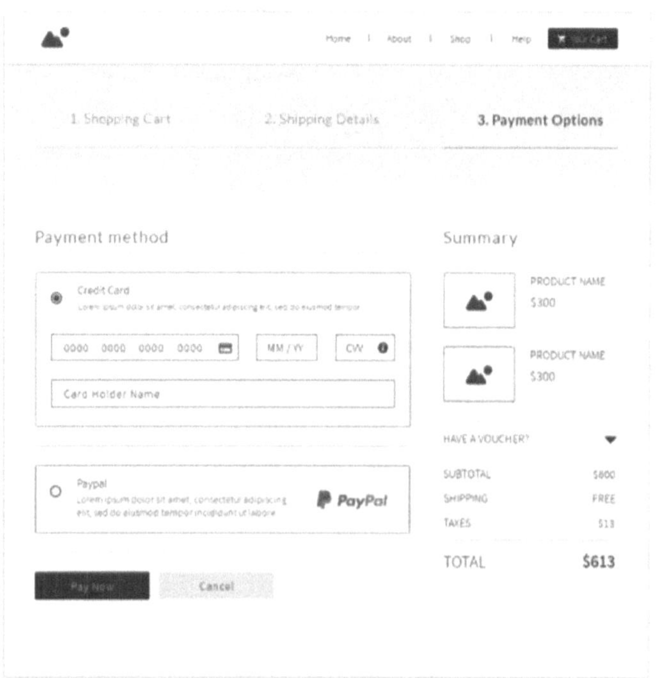

Home | About | Shop | Help
Your Cart
1. Shopping Cart
2. Shipping Details
3. Payment Options
Payment method
Summary
Credit Card
Lorem ipsum dolor sit amet, consectetur adipiscing elit, sed do eiusmod tempor
0000 0000 0000 0000
MM / YY
CVV
Card Holder Name
Paypal
Lorem ipsum dolor sit amet, consectetur adipiscing
elit, sed do eiusmod tempor incididunt ut labore
PayPal
PRODUCT NAME
$300
PRODUCT NAME
$300
HAVE A VOUCHER?
SUBTOTAL
$600
SHIPPING
FREE
TAXES
$13
TOTAL
$613
Pay Now
Cancel

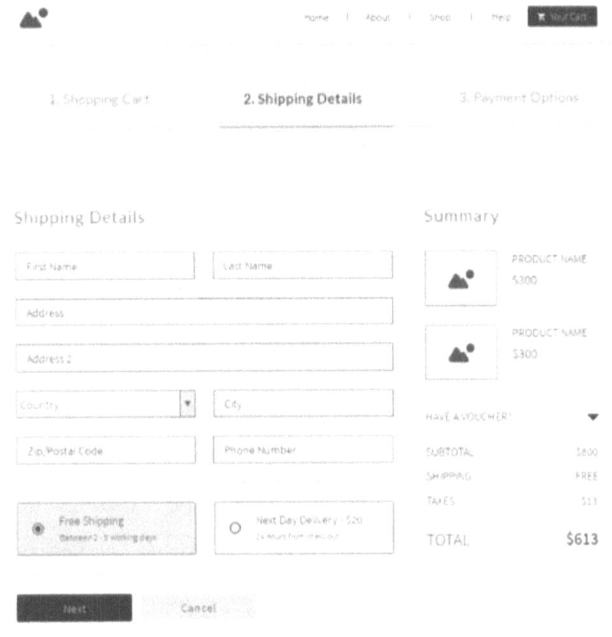
Home | About | Shop | Help | Your Cart
1. Shopping Cart   2. Shipping Details   3. Payment Options
Shipping Details
First Name
Last Name
Address
Address 2
Country
City
Zip/Postal Code
Phone Number
Free Shipping
Between 2 - 3 working days
Next Day Delivery - $20
24 hours from checkout
Next
Cancel
Summary
PRODUCT NAME
$300
PRODUCT NAME
$300
HAVE A VOUCHER?
SUBTOTAL $600
SHIPPING   FREE
TAXES $13
TOTAL $613

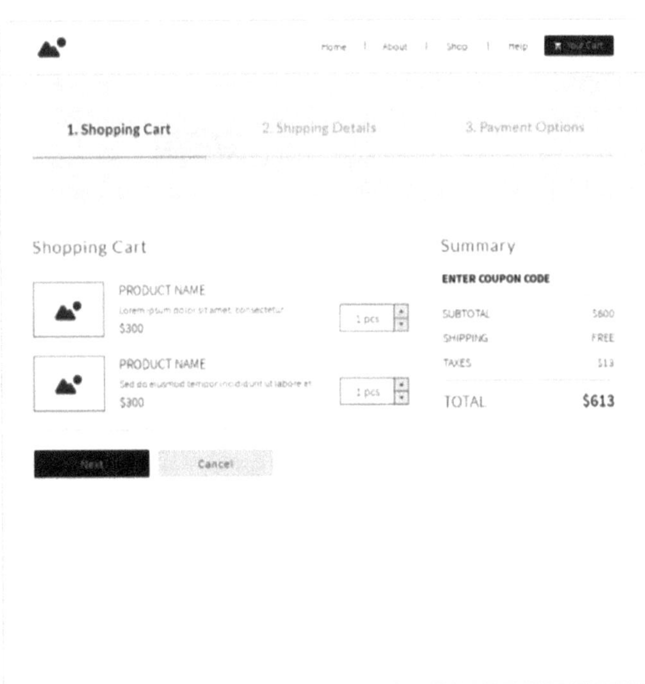
Home | About | Shop | Help | Your Cart
1. Shopping Cart   2. Shipping Details   3. Payment Options
Shopping Cart
PRODUCT NAME
Lorem ipsum dolor sit amet, consectetur
$300
1 pcs
PRODUCT NAME
Sed do eiusmod tempor incididunt ut labore et
$300
1 pcs
Next
Cancel
Summary
ENTER COUPON CODE
SUBTOTAL $600
SHIPPING   FREE
TAXES $13
TOTAL $613

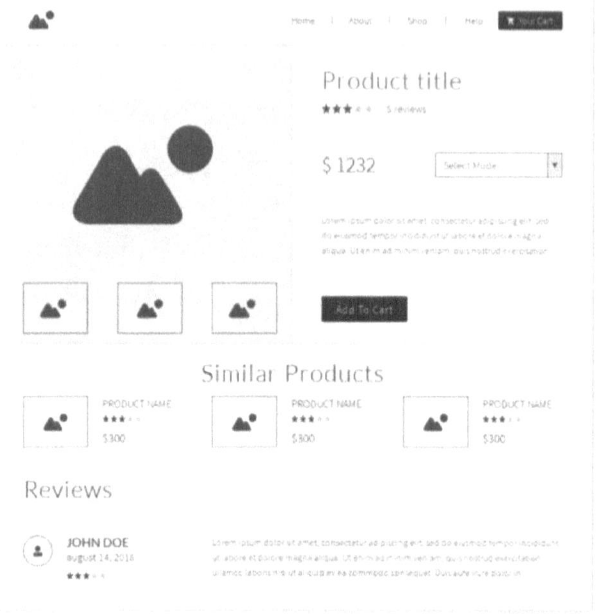

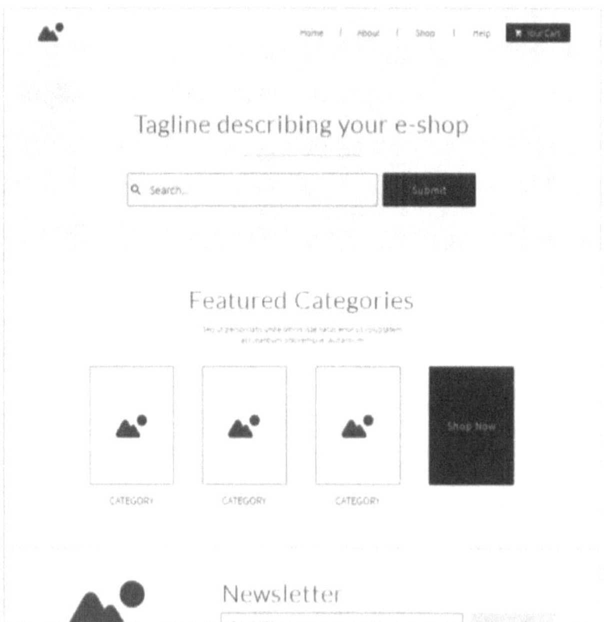

Image Ref : www.moqups.com

User Interface

User Interface is totally about the look and feel of the website/ app. It is best left to a creative UI/UX (User Interface/User Experience) designer or if you are equipped to do this yourself.. nothing like it. . However, as the Founder, you just need to ensure that the deliverable is as per the following :

- Brand colours/typography have to be used as planned, as per the voice of the brand.

- It should be responsive - should not break when viewed on any device, be it mobile, tab or desktop of any resolution

- Simple Interface

- Interactive Interface - Inform the user about actions, change of state or errors

User Journey/User Experience

Presuming you have segmented your Target Audience, it is now time to actually put yourself in the mind of your customer and think how he/she thinks.

There is a very simple process which will help understand what your ideal customer is thinking at each stage of the buying cycle. Accordingly, you can then decide what is the best way to convince him to move to the next stage.

Awareness – What is your ideal target customer thinking when he has just been made aware of your product maybe via a FB ad or an email his friend forwarded him. What other methods can you think about so that you can make him aware about your offering?

Interest – What is your ideal target customer thinking when he has done some research about you and wants to find out more about you? What can you do to ensure you are found on a Google search when he tries to find out about your offering?

Consideration – What is your ideal customer thinking when he has gone ahead and provided his information on your landing page. What is the next step that you must take to ensure you can nurture him to take action and buy your offering?

Action – What is it that will make your customer open up his wallet and pay? How will you make it easy for him to do that?

Fan – How will you make it easy for your customer to recommend you to someone else he knows who can use the same offering?

So you know who your target customer is now, you have actually given them a name and not only that you also know how they think at each stage of the purchase process for your product.

App Development

If you are a software developer yourself and have the confidence and the ability to build the app that you have visualised, that is the best thing to do since it will save you a hell of a lot of money. However, it will take up too much of your time, which will increase your Go-To-Market time. If you are in no particular hurry to launch then this is the best way forward for you.

If you are not technically capable of developing it yourself then outsourcing the development is the only option. You can outsource the development to someone from your network or you can use outsourcing marketplaces like www.fiverr.com or www.upwork.com to do the job. After all you have created the wireframe and visualised the whole concept, all that they have to do is to develop it to make it tangible.

Common Modules

All websites and apps are of course specific to the business. But here are some common modules in a basic product website.

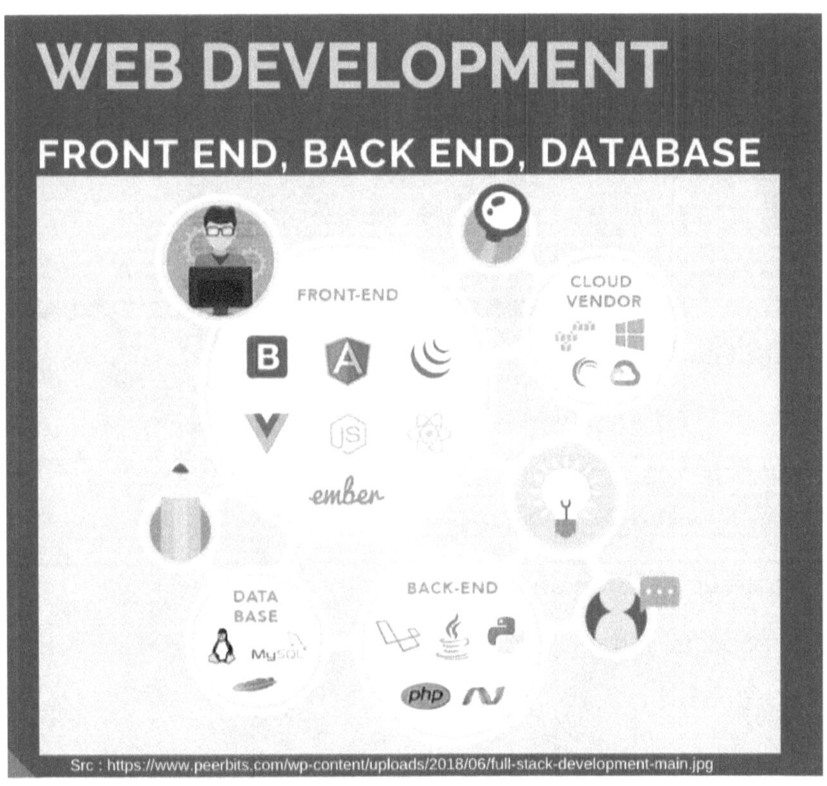

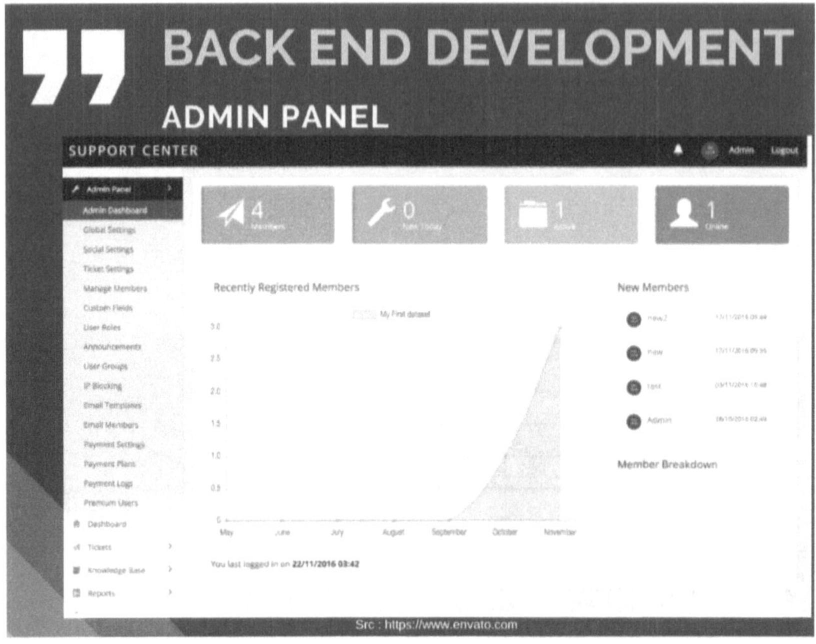

- Front end

  - Register/Login/My Account

  - Browse Categories

  - Loyalty Points Program

  - Referral Program

  - Special Offers

  - Related Offers

  - User Generated Reviews

  - Wishlist

  - Search

  - Blog

  - KnowledgeBase

- Admin Panel
    - Register/Login/My Account
    - Departments like Marketing, Management, Logistics
    - Access Levels like Super Admin, Admin etc
    - Manage Complete Database
    - View Department/Level specific Dashboards and Reports

In how much time will you do this?!- Project Estimation

A year and still not there yet! As the project manager, technical architect, CTO , Fintoo (I was everything built into one) sometime in 2016 I felt the pain of the development team not being able to match the goals they set for themselves. Estimations were heading north and actuals were heading south! Thus came the urge to bring my team on to the agile bandwagon since the experts seemed to say that would solve my problems.

Along came Mike Cohn and became an integral part of my life for the next few days. Learned so much from his book Agile Estimating and Planning. I thought I had finally conquered the world! I immediately ordered Planning Poker cards from Amazon and went on the next day totally charged up to tell the team that we are going on an exciting journey from here on!

We were in the conference room sitting with yummy breakfast on the table, each team member with a deck of cards in their hands, with pale expressions on their faces wondering why are we playing a game on a fresh Monday morning ! Soon I explained things, the team started story point estimation on the user stories which I had struggled with and created over the weekend. At first it took a lot of time for me to explain to them what the story point meant. T-Shirt sizes, buckets .. I used all the techniques that Mike taught me to make them understand what relative estimation means! I literally had to tear them away from their habit of estimating in hours. No matter how hard I tried they kept going back to hours. Found them a middle solution where I told them they can do both. Estimate in hours and estimate in story points both for some sprints and then we would reach a point where we could slowly move away from hours to story points completely.

It's more than a year since that lovely Monday morning and the team still estimates both! Finally after a lot of brainstorming with the Project Manager and a series of sprint burndown reports which showed the estimated story point line going down exponentially very neatly but the actual burndown refusing to tilt down (in fact sometimes going in the opposite direction due to our failure to avoid scope creep) , we decided it was high time we go back to the Monday morning breakfast table and chalk things out again!

Henry Ford comforted me …

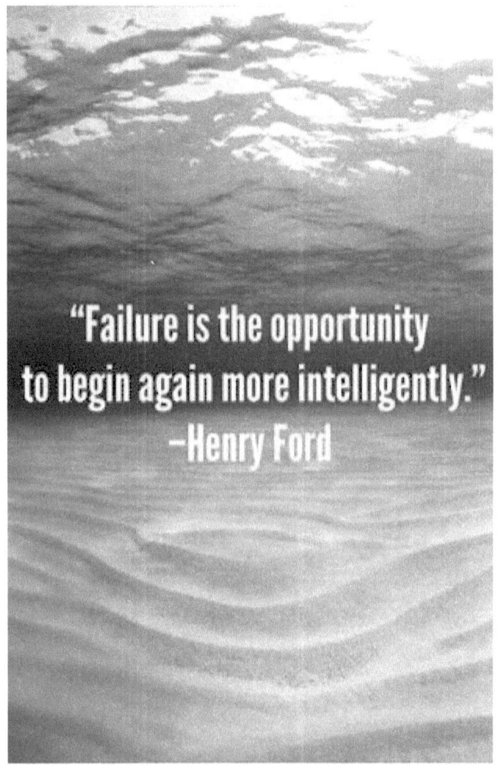

.. and so here I am comforting the team and myself that we will start again, this time with lunch included on the menu!

Let's start all over again Spent my weekend this time trying to do all the groundwork so that I could wrap this up on Monday nice and easy! Was highly unsuccessful at trying to establish the velocity of my team earlier. The earlier sprints showed velocity of 20 sometimes and 120 sometimes (there was one which had a velocity of 0) , so averaging that would make no sense. Did some research on first sprint planning and came across a very good idea. We had to start somewhere so it was important to establish some benchmark for velocity. I had sworn I wouldn't let the habit of hourly estimation come in. It was going to be story point estimation all the way! These were some basic calculations which gave me a starter..

Worked out some Examples of user stories and their story points (Including testing and bug efforts)

- Login – 1
- Investment Account – Personal details – 3
- Investment Account – KYC – 5
- View Portfolio – Asset Drill down – 8
- View Portfolio – Transaction Listing – 13
- View Portfolio – Bank Balance Integration – 21

This magic calculation thrilled me and gave me a good starting point and hope for a better future for my team

- Developers – 4
- Sprint length – 10
- 1 Story point – 1 hr (0.125 days)
- Developer Focus Factor (meeting et al.) – 60%
- Total person days – 40
- Ideal person days – 24
- Story points in ideal person days – 24*0.125 = 192
- Story points per developer – 48

The fact that I could estimate that each of my developers (with the testers) could complete approximately 48 story points in a sprint was enough confidence for me and the team that we would pull it off successfully this time since we had some benchmark to start this time!

It's not about you, it's about the user story!

Some arguments and conflicts which I have faced in the past and expect to come up on this Monday are .. "bugs take up so much time, why aren't you letting me estimate them to.. after all the story points indicate my effort!" My answer "a bug is a slip from your end, your Karma, so don't call it your effort ".. rude but true, they got to agree! Tester says "what about my effort.. I am nowhere in the story point estimation for the test tasks that i create". My answer "it's about taking the user story to completion. You may include your effort in the story points estimated for that user story ". The tester also says "I will be sitting idle till these guys give me the user stories to test, and at the end they all sit on my head when their development is done, each asking me to test his user story first!" My answer "The day the user stories are defined and moved to the current sprint, that day your work starts on developing the test cases for their user stories. It is possible that you may be ready with their test cases even before they finish developing it!. That's actually the right way to go!"

At the end of it all my friends, it's not about you as the developer or the tester.. it's about the user story!

Future perfect!

So, this is what we will do on Monday..

- * Move pending issues from last sprint to backlog

- * Close last sprint

- * Arrange user stories in order of priority for each developer

- * Assign assignee, version, epic, component, estimate, due date time, story points

- * For each user story create (if not exists) test task for the same and link test task to user story

- * Arrange test tasks in order of priority of user stories

- * Move user stories matching with the estimated velocity to new sprint

If all goes well and the Gods are by our side then , here's looking forward to a future perfect scenario. We estimate user stories on story points always, we arrive at an average velocity over the next few sprints, we move work worth the velocity to the current sprint and away we go on a happy ride down the perfect sprint burndown chart!

Data Privacy Guidelines

Everyone is concerned about data security and privacy but technology-dependent businesses have even more to worry about.

Here are six solutions that will help startups ensure data security and privacy without high costs:

1. Prevent data sharing in any way

Consumer cloud file sync/share tools significantly increase the risk of data breaches if not implemented properly. As a result, employees often unknowingly introduce risk to a company by simply syncing data across their devices, working with others outside the organisation. Your IT department must be proactively involved to prevent these data breaches and address them when they occur. There are options available to lock USB drives to prevent any data copy on an external device.

2. Create a data security policy

At a minimum, every company must establish data security policies that include guidelines for file sharing. A company should identify the critical assets of its business and be clear about where they are stored, whether they are encrypted, and who has the keys.

Your website/app should not collect protected information from customers and employees unless they truly need it for operations. Similarly, information that is no longer needed must be destroyed.

3. Train employees

The most important thing any company can do to protect itself from a data breach is to spend a significant amount of time and money on training their team to avoid cyber attacks. Employee training should include data loss prevention, social engineering identification, least privileged access, physical security of devices, creating a reliable and secure password, and identifying suspicious links and attachments from phishing attacks.

4. Cloud for data storage

A simple and easy solution for startups is to store their data on a cloud solution that can incorporate data-centric security as well as application-level security, where the security measures are embedded in the data itself as opposed to protecting only the infrastructure. It makes sense to leverage experts and vendors to get access to sophisticated and compliant tools such as Amazon Web Services (AWS), Dropbox, Box, Salesforce, etc.

5. Encrypt, especially your sensitive data

One of the most cost-effective ways a startup company can protect itself from a data breach is encryption. And encrypting not just sensitive information — like credit card numbers or social security numbers, which are non-negotiable — but all information, like email addresses, is essential.

6. Conduct penetration testing and vulnerability testing regularly

Penetration and Vulnerability testing involves using tools and techniques which try to break the system in an ethically hacking approach to find faults and breaches and address them. This can also be outsourced to a team which specialises in the same.

There are a number of penetration testing tools available in every price range. It is worth it to spend some money and time to identify your company's specific needs and find a specific tool that will address your business needs and be manageable to operate.

7. Data Backup and Recovery

Ensure there are regular backups to avoid data loss and minimum recovery time in case of database failure.

Workshop

Habit Forming Perspective

Create the documentation for the Habit Forming Perspective from your target customer's point of view using this template - https://links.thegreycells.com/HabitForming

Mind Map

Create a mind map using www.justinmind.com or any other tool of your choice -

Use this template as a reference. - https://links.thegreycells.com/MindMap

MVP

Arrive at a minimum Viable Plan using the Product Plan Template - https://links.thegreycells.com/ProductPlan

Paper Prototype

Take a pen and paper and create a paper prototype which will be used as a reference base by your development team.

Use this template as a reference. - https://links.thegreycells.com/PaperPrototype

Wireframe

Create a wireframe using www.figma.com or www.moqups.com or any other tool of your choice -

Use this template as a reference. - https://links.thegreycells.com/Wireframe

Templates

- https://links.thegreycells.com/HabitForming
- https://links.thegreycells.com/MindMap
- https://links.thegreycells.com/ProductPlan
- https://links.thegreycells.com/PaperPrototype
- https://links.thegreycells.com/Wireframe

Chapter 11

Step 5 - Marketing, Sales, Post-Sales

Frugality is the new mantra for Startup Success.

Whether you are self-funded or externally funded. The core values must be the same. To ensure minimal spend and maximum profits.

And without any doubt, based on my real experience I can say confidently that the biggest guzzler where Startup expenses are concerned is the Marketing Spend. Or let me be more specific, Paid Marketing Spend.

I will be quick to add here that I am not saying it is not needed. The kind of traffic and conversion boost that Paid Marketing can get, no amount of organic marketing can do the same. What is needed however, is a fine balance between Organic (Zero Cost) and Paid Marketing.

Agenda :

- Funnel Setup
- Zero Cost Organic Marketing
  - Rich Content Creation

- Systematic Content Scheduling
- Customised Content
- Guest Posting
- Social Media Marketing
- Audience Engagement
- Search Engine Optimisation (SEO)
- App Store Optimisation (ASO)
- Marketing Automation
- Paid Marketing
- How to determine your Product Pricing
- How to determine your Marketing Budget
- Marketing Analytics (What gets measured gets managed)
- Post Sales (Customer Service)

Funnel Setup

Image Ref : https://www.leadsquared.com

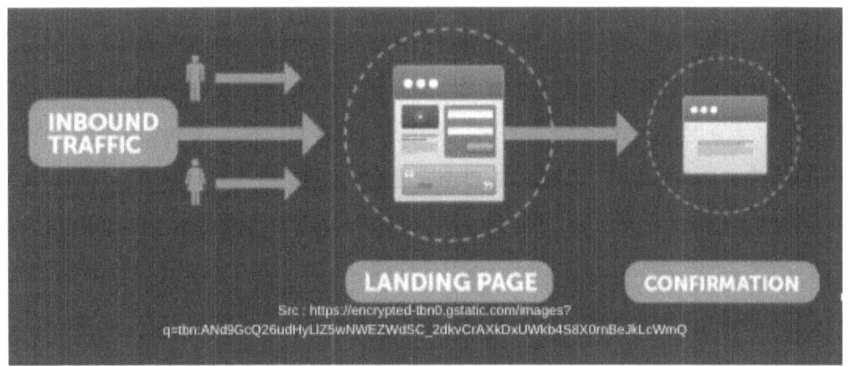

https://links.thegreycells.com/Funnel

https://links.thegreycells.com/FunnelMapping

Zero Cost Organic Marketing

Rich Content Creation

Content is king. Heard about this a number of times.

What is important to understand is what exactly can be classified as "rich" content. According to me, there is only one definition. Rich Content = Targeted Content.

If your audience cannot relate to what you are writing, if it does not instil curiosity to click the CTA (Call-To-Action) to find out more, then the content is plain useless. Yes, we are here to create awareness for our customers, but let's admit, the bottomline is to sell. Not at the first rung of the ladder, but at the last rung, when your content has generated sufficient curiosity to inspire a sale.

There are many good articles about what kind of content you should post so I won't go deep into that. There is a link in the references which will help you with that.

What is important is to understand what will work for your brand and what won't. Just because memes are popular doesn't mean you post all content in the form of memes. If there is a need for long form content like blogs for your audience to understand what your brand is really about, then you go to do it, even if it involves more time and energy. On the other hand, if your product is on the creative side, then illustrative content may generate more engagement than a blog.

You have a very limited span of attention on social media. Make the most of it, by generating Rich Content/Target Content

Systematic Content Scheduling

How often should a Startup post content? This is a very common question. And yet again, there are many articles which tell you what you should do. You can find a link in the references which tells you the best practices for how many times you should post and at what times to post.

Cool, so now you know how much and when to post. All this needs to be put up somewhere in Black and White in the form of a Content Calendar to ensure execution happens as planned. It may sound easy, but it needs to be smartly scheduled and planned to ensure just the right balance between awareness and nagging.

Another aspect is, ensuring that your Content Writer is delivering content on time so that it is posted as per the schedule you have defined above. As a best practice, I give a deadline to the content writers to deliver the content 3 days before it is scheduled to be posted.

Here is a handy content calendar that I have developed over the years to not only plan posting but controlling the entire pipeline from content creation to creative development to final posting.

https://links.thegreycells.com/ContentCalendar

Social Media Marketing

What I would like to point out here, specifically, is the voice of social media content that goes out. Remember, **each channel has its own voice.** What you post on FB may not necessarily generate engagement on Instagram. If that was the case FB would not have bought Instagram. Instagram is more about Stories and Reels. So post the same content in that format.

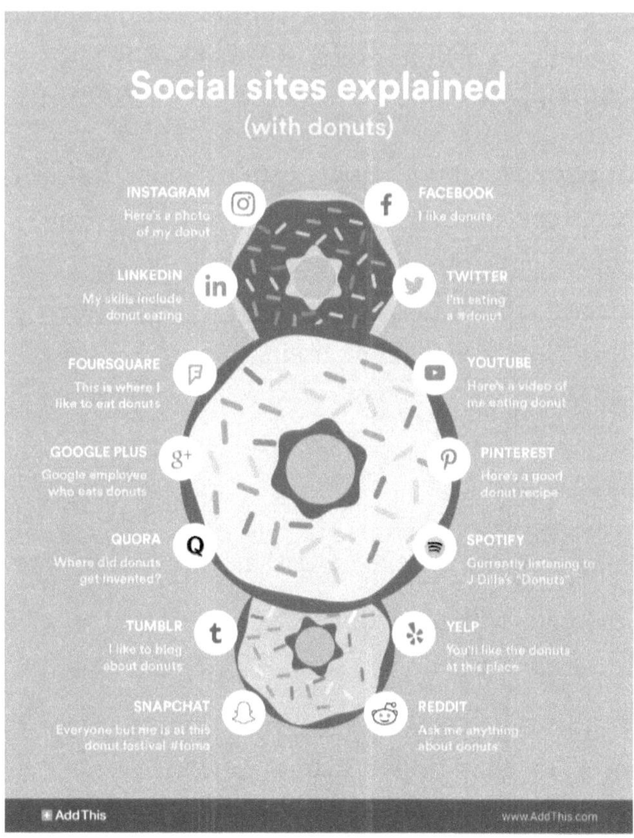

https://blog.addthiscdn.com/wp-content/uploads/2015/09/11234656/
Donuts-01-1-808x1024.png

We all do it to save time. I admit I do too. And that is all the more reason that I am stressing here that it is a big mistake. It is a waste of good content.

Guest Posting

I'll define Guest Posting in crude terms. It is piggybacking on someone else's popularity 😊. However, crude it may sound, there is nothing wrong with it. All is fair in love and digital marketing.

Here's the thing – Maybe you are starting off while some other website in your niche (not a direct competitor but a related entity to your domain of work) has been there and generated some good traffic for themselves.

Everyone needs good content to draw traffic but not everyone has good content writers. Here's how you can create a win-win scenario out of this. Those who are looking for good content will generally create a form on their website inviting guest posts. You can offer your expertise for the same.

How will this help you?

In many ways :

- You come across as an expert in that domain for their readers

- Some of them will allow limited link backs to your site, which will increase traffic on your site.

- If you are really good you have the potential to become an influencer in that domain and generate a separate income stream out of it

- You bring in new audience from various sources instead of just your own.

- You expand your network by connecting to related businesses in your domain and you can tap the potential to increase your offerings by including their services in your basket in the form of a collaboration

Audience Engagement

This has been the biggest pain point for me. In terms of explaining the importance of engaging with your potential Audience to all Startups whom I have consulted.

No matter how much content you post, if you cannot get engagement on it, it is not worth anything. When I say engagement it would even mean simple Likes and Shares. Comments would really take it to another level altogether.

Posting the content on your social media channels is equivalent to putting up a poster inside your shop. Those who walk in will see the poster, but then they are already probably in, so you can convince them anyway. Post your content in Social Media Groups and post it logically. Maybe as a comment in response to a similar post.

A secret technique that works very well is posting your content in response to a question on Quora. The intent of content should not be publicity or sales. Write content to serve a need genuinely. And in the end, even if you close it with a promotion, no one minds, because you helped them in some little way.

Search Engine Optimisation (SEO)

SEO (Search Engine Optimisation) sounds so technical that the non-techie Startup Founders try to stay away or try to delay initiating that activity for their Startup Product.

Mark my words, it is the easiest and best way to ensure you hold your purse strings tight on the Marketing Spend.

All it needs is a) identifying the correct keywords related to your business and b) using those keywords intelligently and logically in the content that you post. What this will ensure is that whenever someone is searching for those keywords in Google your content will be ranked high on the SERP (Search Engine Result Pages), thereby increasing the likelihood of a prospect reading your content and clicking the CTA (Call To Action).

This technique takes time to show results, but you can clearly see it can get you sales for Zero Marketing Spend.

- On-Page
  - Title Tag, Headings
  - Keyword Density
  - Improve Page Speed
  - Decrease Bounce Rate
- Off-Page
  - Backlinks

GOAL FOR SEO : TRAFFIC

App Store Optimisation (ASO)

This is all about improving the ranking for your mobile app on App Store and Google Play (which have their own dedicated search engines) and also on Google (by using a technique called deep linking)

- On-Page
  - App Name, Description
  - Keywords
  - Usage and quality metrics
  - Decrease Uninstall Rate
- Off-Page
  - Backlinks
  - Ratings
  - Reviews
  - Download Stats

GOAL FOR ASO : APP DOWNLOADS

Marketing Automation

The power of automation in general is highly underestimated. The power of Marketing Automation – more so.

Not only is it underestimated, it is also misused.

The general thought process is – let's get huge volumes of email ids and phone numbers and let's use marketing automation to blast the life out of them. Unfortunately, that results in nothing. In fact, that can be detrimental to the health of the email list you have built with so much effort (and probably money). An unengaged email list makes your email id a victim of the spam brigade. The more your marketing list is unengaged the more are the chances that the next email your email will land up in your customer's spam accounts.

Here's the thing – Instead of blasting out periodic broadcast posts to the entire list, what is needed as a Best Practice for Marketing Automation is a defined process. Something, which I have termed as ANO (Acquire -> Nurture -> Offer).

https://links.thegreycells.com/MarketerBot

This is a carefully crafted process which I have created over the years after meticulous observation of how a customer moves from Awareness to an Ambassador of your product.

Acquire

It all starts with a magic potion called "Lead Magnet".

Lead Magnet – Another Marketing Jargon?

A Lead Magnet is a goodie that you propose to give out to your audience with a subtle selfish aim. Nothing wrong with that. All you are asking for is their email id and/or phone number. This will ensure you can keep knocking on their doors on the pretext of reminding them that you exist and maybe one fine day it dawns upon them that they need what you create.

How a Lead Magnet can change the way you market

The main advantage that a Lead Magnet can offer you is establish you as an expert in your field. And once you have done that, it is smooth sailing from there on since the initial trust is established.

Also, you are sure that you will have a genuine lead since the person is actually parting away with his/her precious email id so that they can get a piece of valuable knowledge from you. Buying email lists with ids of people unknown to you and vice versa does not serve any purpose.

The easily shareable nature of Lead Magnets have the extra advantage of your voice reaching out to tons of others in the network of that single person who found your knowledge of value.

What kind of Lead Magnets work

The most common lead magnet since time immemorial has been an EBook. Here's an awesome EBook which will change your life! Well, all you need to do is give me your email id and I will send it to you by email. This still works. But with a disclaimer.

Just creating an EBook out of the blue and expecting people to give away their precious email ids to use it is not going to work. The most important aspect of the EBook is the title. That is the deal breaker. There are Headline Analyser tools which can help you with that.

How engaging the content and design are also matter of course, but it is the title that is going to entice the user to give their email in return for the knowledge that you are sharing.

Make sure that your EBook provides instant gratification to the reader by solving one single real problem that is the biggest pain point in their life at that point in time.

Let's accept it. People are bored of downloading EBooks. Some other good lead magnets which can fulfil the goal of acquiring and onboarding a visitor are :

- Surveys
- Book A Consultation
- Get a Callback
- Online Event Invitation (Webinar)
- Subscribe to Knowledge Base (Blog, Podcast, YouTube Channel)
- Product Demo
- Product Free Trial
- Contests
- Special Offers
- Templates
- Chatbots/Live Chats

All it requires to create an engaging lead magnet is a little bit of imagination by putting yourself in your target customer's shoes and a little bit of innovation to create something that inspires action.

Nurture

Onboarding a prospective customer is the beginning of a new relationship. It has to be nurtured with utmost care using Marketing Automation to achieve the perfect balance between providing valuable information and not nagging them.

There are many marketing tools that you can use to achieve this purpose. Some of the popular ones are listed below :

- Zoho Marketing Automation
- Kajabi
- ConvertKit

- Active Campaign

- Hubspot

- Aweber

A good way of keeping in touch with prospective customers and at the same time building their trust is a Drip Campaign.

A Drip Campaign is a series of emails that you send over a couple of days as a Knowledge Campaign related to the subject of interest based on which they signed up with you. Each day a capsule of information with a build up on the same over the next day can get them interested in a subtle non-invasive way.

On the last day, when you pitch subtly by sending a product trial , it can spark interest because there is already a relationship built there because of the nurturing that you have done over the past couple of days using the Drip Campaign.

If you have provided valuable information in the Drip Campaign , a nudge here and there to subscribe to your social media channels would ensure they keep getting updates all the while. At the last leg of a marketing journey I make sure to drop in a Keep In Touch mailer if the prospect has not shown interest in the Drip Campaign. This Keep In Touch mailer has a link to all my social media channels.

The bottomline in this stage is to Serve , not to Sell. Have the selfless approach there and when they are ready to buy they will come to you even if you are not pitching to them at that point in time.

Offer

Now that the initial trust is established, it's time to introduce your offer.

Sell

Make sure you package it up with a good deal which is really hard to refuse. Nothing works as well as a Free Trial or a Free Demo. Free is a not a bad word if it is used as Freemium. Everyone knows that if they use it for Free there will be some kind of upsell down the line and they should be ok with that as long as what you are providing for Free has some tangible value.

Upsell

So, finally you got your prospect interested, made them loosen their purse strings and pay for your Level 1 product. Time to Upsell..

If your Level 1 product has really provided value, it's time for a nurture campaign for Level 2 products. Gather feedback, ensure that Level 1 delivered what it promised to deliver and then pitch Level 2.

Finally it's all about service. If you provide good after sales support for Level 1 and Level 2 now makes sense to the customer, he/she will surely opt for Level 2.

A good offer here because of the loyalty factor will help push the Upsell more effectively.

Cross Sell

This can be used in 2 ways.

If the prospect did not show an interest in Level 1, then you can pitch Level 1A which is an alternative option for Level 1 (maybe cheaper). Or maybe Level 1A is more suited to the customer than Level 1 even though its price may be higher.

In any case the key here is to send a customised journey of emails based on preference selection in the first stage. Personalisation can reach out in a way that inspires action because the prospect can relate to it closely.

Another good reason to cross-sell another product could be that a customer bought Level 1 and Level 1A adds on value to Level 1. An example could be an accessory that goes with Level 1. The "You might also need" option on Amazon and other popular ecommerce sites is a great example of that. Sending that out in an email after the customer has bought Level 1 might just result in a sale since it is a personalised offering that will add value to his/her recent purchase.

Resell/Renew

Perfectly coordinated systems which maintain data intelligence, play a very important role in this process.

This aspect of the business can be completely automated by setting reminders, initiating marketing on triggers and following up with a journey till the renewal is completed.

At the last stage, a subtle phone call as a reminder, is not a nagging thing, since all you are doing is your duty by reminding them to continue the subscription (if there is one)

https://links.thegreycells.com/MarketerBotTemplates

So, this is what you need to do to get started :

- Create an automation journey based on the MarketerBot (Acquire-Nurture-Offer) Formula using any tool like Zoho Marketing Automation

- Fill in the Blanks in the Email Templates. Pre-Built content ready to be filled in with your company specific information

- Configure and start Automation. Integrate the emails and the journey in the tool and start automation

Paid Marketing

Paid Marketing is a clear input-output phenomenon. Put in the money and see the traffic flowing.

Well of course you have to do it in the right way otherwise you can end up losing a lot of money.

Also, although you might hear it a lot, Facebook Ads are not the only answer to Paid Marketing. Each business has its own voice and its own target customers which reside on various different social networks. Identify where they reside and spend money to run ads there.

If you want to learn the techniques of paid marketing there are tons of courses available out there. I recommend the ones by www.nikswami.com . If you have never really got your hands wet there then I recommend you outsource this to someone reliable on www.fiverr.com or www.upwork.com

Src : https://wunderboom.files.wordpress.com/2018/05/paid-advertising-services.png?w=816

Paid Marketing Process

Src : http://www.digiwebart.com/wp-content/uploads/2019/05/Online-Advertising-Agency.jpg

How to determine your product pricing

It is often said Product Pricing is an art as much as it is a science. Well, I beg to differ.

I would clearly say that it is better to treat product pricing as a science since it is directly related to your revenue. Keep your creative side aside and rely on the formula and logic rather than the gut feeling.

Following are some logical best practices or thumb rules to follow when you sit down to brainstorm your product price.

- All prices must cover costs.

- The most effective way to lower prices is to lower costs.

- Review prices frequently to assure that they reflect the dynamics of cost, market demand, response to the competition, and profit objectives.

- Prices must be established to assure sales initially (to achieve Break-Even) and then to gradually start getting in profits.

Let's look at the various pricing models :

- Cost Based Pricing
  - Selling Price = Cost Price + Profit
  - Profit Margin is generally taken as 50% to start off with.
  - So,
    - if you have spent Rs. 200 in manufacturing a product,
    - then you take profit as 50% of 200 = Rs. 100
    - and so you sell the product for Rs. 200 + Rs. 100 = Rs. 300

- Market (Competitor Based Pricing)
  - Check what price your competitors are offering for the same product. Either price slightly higher than them, or equal to what they are charging or lower than them
- Dynamic Pricing
  - Change prices as per season.
  - E.g. Amazon
- Discount Pricing
  - Offer discount percentage on the actual price to entice the customer to buy due to FOMO
- Loss Leader Pricing
  - Sell some products at a loss with the expectation that the customer will surely buy some other associated products on which you have higher profit margin thereby compensating the loss.
- Anchor Pricing
  - State the regular price in the market.
  - Offer a lower price than that.

When should you review and refurbish prices :

- You introduce a new product or product line;
- Your costs change;
- You decide to enter a new market;
- Your competitors change their prices;
- The economy experiences either inflation or recession;
- Your sales strategy changes; or

- Your customers are making more money because of your product or service.

How to determine your Marketing Budget

https://links.thegreycells.com/MarketingBudget

NOTE : WE WILL BE DOING THIS ACTIVITY AT ONE GO ALONG WITH THE OTHER EXPENSE AND REVENUE PROJECTIONS ACTIVITY IN THE STEP 7 : FUNDING.

Marketing Analytics (What gets measured gets managed)

https://links.thegreycells.com/MarketingMetrics

Post Sales (Customer Service)

Tool : Zoho Desk

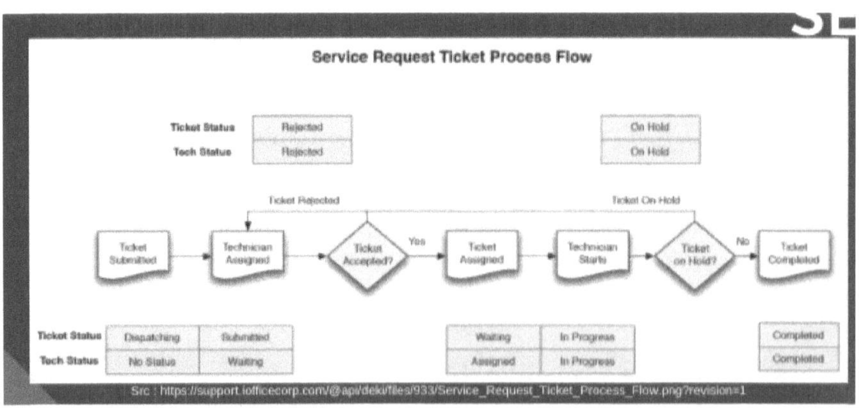

Workshop

Funnel Definitions

Define your Funnels using the Acquire -> Nurture -> Offer Formula.

Use these templates

- https://links.thegreycells.com/Funnel
- https://links.thegreycells.com/FunnelMapping
- https://links.thegreycells.com/MarketerBot
- https://links.thegreycells.com/MarketerBotTemplates

Content Calendar

Create your content marketing strategy and schedule in a content calendar using this template

- https://links.thegreycells.com/ContentCalendar

Remember to incorporate keywords which you identified in the Week 2 - Step 2 - Startup Idea Validation using the Idea Validator Framework using this template - https://links.thegreycells.com/KeywordResearch

Product Pricing

Determine your product/service price(s) using the Pricing Models explained.

Marketing Budget

Prepare your marketing budget by taking a measured guess on the value of the number of customers. You can update this later when you work out the TAM, SAM , SOM in the Step 7 - Fund Raising Session.

Use this template - https://links.thegreycells.com/MarketingBudget

Templates

- https://links.thegreycells.com/Funnel
- https://links.thegreycells.com/FunnelMapping
- https://links.thegreycells.com/ContentCalendar
- https://links.thegreycells.com/MarketerBot
- https://links.thegreycells.com/MarketerBotTemplates
- https://links.thegreycells.com/MarketingBudget

References

- https://blog.hubspot.com/marketing/content-marketing-types
- https://blog.hubspot.com/marketing/how-frequently-should-i-publish-on-social-media
- https://links.thegreycells.com/MarketingMetrics

Digital Marketing – Ask Me Anything (FAQ)

Entrepreneurship is not easy. To some it comes naturally, to some it's a learning along the way. My personal opinion is that whether it comes to you naturally or you learn along the way, ultimately it is a series of processes that you follow to make your dream turn into reality. While you follow those processes, you find answers to your problems at hand and you carve the path to your success. And to each his own!

Along this journey of Entrepreneurship, I have been asked many questions by aspiring Entrepreneurs. Here are some of them, which even gave me an insight into some things which I had not always known but researched just to help these people out to the best of my capabilities.

How to measure ROI on online marketing?

- What do you measure
  - Traffic (Unique)

- CPL (cost per lead)
- CPA (Cost per acquisition)
- ROAS (return on ad spend)
- CLTV (Customer Lifetime Value)
- Ranking
- Calculations
  - I am a big advocate of using tools. Google Analytics is good but gives you traffic , ad conversions very well. But if you need a consolidated view of your ads, social media, Search engine traffic etc. using a tool like Zoho One or Hubspot makes a lot more sense.
  - Zoho allows you to plan your paid marketing. Specify your target budget, captures your actual ad spends and gives you ROI
  - But then there are other expenses like what you pay for content development, marketing tools. That has to be taken in separately for the final ROI.

Is short form content better or long form content?
- Long form content is content which is > 2000 words
- Depends on
  - Product
    - Some products have extensive documentation e.g. a marketing tool, B2B product.
    - Till you convince the user that it is easy to use he will not buy from you. There you need ebooks, white-papers, infographics – long form content.
    - Also brings you across as an expert

- Some products like an online shop don't have complex processes. So you can just pitch and sell – short form content
- User Intent
  - If the user is just at the awareness stage you need long form content to make him understand well about your product
  - When the user is deeper down in the funnel, a short clear pitch is good enough to sell
- Channel
  - Social media – short form – people have less time
  - SEO – Long form with keywords
- Bottomline

How to sell products on Whatsapp alone?

- 20 cr people use whatsapp so its a big medium
- How to sell
  - Get a Whatsapp business number
    - Can be landline number also
    - Business name
    - Publish it everywhere
    - Different from personal or convert if u want to sell to your personal contact
  - How is it different from whatsapp
    - You have to install the Whatsapp Business App which is a different app
    - Business Profile Settings

- Verified seller – so trust is established
- Product Catalogue can be exhibited
- Auto reply (Using Automation)
- Greeting and Away Message
- Quick Replies – define a keyword and a message for frequently used messages
- Where to sell
  - Known contacts/groups
  - Whatsapp selling groups
    - Find them by
    - asking someone who is selling (who has sent you a message),
    - groups on FB where people are selling – they must be part of these whatsapp seller groups
    - websites which list whatsapp seller groups – Groupya
    - create your own group
- Payments
  - Whatsapp payments
  - Other payment apps like PayTM, PhonePe
- Pricing
  - Messaging is free
  - API – connect to your systems – may be chargeable
  - reminders, tickets, order delivery through your apps
    - Twilio
  - They structured their pricing in such a way that it will cost money only when a business responds to clients

messages beyond 24 hours. All messages that were responded to, within a 24 hours period are free. Beyond that, they would cost anywhere between 5 cents to 90 cents for sending response messages. Or In Indian rupees we can say around 4 rupees – 60 Rupees roughly.

Video vs Images?

- Hands down – Video – as per statistics
  - Youtube is now a dedicated video search engine in itself. Optimising your video searches for relevant keywords is the sure-shot way to success.
- Webinars and Facebook YouTube Live shows have maximum visibility.
- Automated Webinars (Pre-Recorded Webinars) are for those product owners who cannot find a suitable time to connect with all their audience. The webinar can be pre-recorded and posted at a given time. Questions can be replied to then and there if you are available or later.
- Sometimes an image says it all – infographic

Zero cost online marketing tips

- SEO (Search Engine Optimisation)
  - Takes time but content driven so good quality leads
  - Backlinks from influencers, partner websites, barter
  - User generated content (comments)
- Effective Social Media Marketing
- Community Engagement
  - Social Media Groups
  - Forums like Quora, Reddit

- Cross promote (up-sell)
- Guest blogging
- Commenting
- Help a Reporter Out (HARO)
- Free Press Releases
- In-person networking
- Referral program
- Influencer marketing
    - Sometimes this comes with a cost, but if you also have something to contribute some influencers appreciate that and don't charge you.
- Grow your email list
- Organic Youtube marketing
    - Optimise your video descriptions with relevant keywords
    - Engage with audience

Do FB stores really help with sales?

- Shop from within FB
- Integrate shopify or any other existing ecommerce store
- FB Ads integrated
- FB Stories for featured products
- Tagging
- Reviews
- Insights
- If your audience is on FB (B2C) then it would help in a great way

What are the pros and cons to create a Whatsapp business account?

- Pros
  - Mentioned above
- Cons
  - Security – always there in the back of the mind
  - Cant mix personal and professional

Can you give insights on the few best free tools available to manage all social media handles?

- Zoho Social
- Hootsuite
- Buffer
- All of these have basic versions as free but as you scale you have to pay which you wouldn't mind if you can still effectively be in positive ROI since you are scaling

How to use digital marketing effectively for Edtech or other software products ?

- Let's take the example of an Online Course Marketplace
- Paid Ads for drawing in the traffic on your website or landing pages will come in handy of course at the initial level.
- The funnel for Edtech focuses a lot on awareness in terms of what you are going to teach in the courses that you provide, what is the benefit of learning that course, and interesting articles about the course topic. So the key has to be to get users interested and make them understand that the course is beneficial for them. So content marketing (pdfs, ebooks, white-papers etc) will play a big role for the top end of the funnel and

make you come across as an expert in your field for people to trust you and your brand.

- If you have good content, your SEO will anyway have a strong base to make you rank well for your industry related keywords.

- Social Media will play a role in Customer Retention where you interact with enrolled students – provide customer support and up-sell other courses where you see scope

- Quora and Reddit are excellent channels for projecting yourself as an expert. Go and answer questions on Quora, solve people's problems and see how people are drawn to you and your brand.

Do you think Digital Marketing is effective in acquiring customers for fintech and investment platforms? I have a feeling that the CAC is high?

- The CAC would really depend on the kind of Fintech product that you are selling. For e.g if you are selling insurance the CAC is way beyond reach for any Small or Medium Fintech player. That's because there are huge Insurance companies who will anyway be ranked topmost almost always if we talk about SEO. However, if you talk about a product like Wealth Advisory the competition as of today is not that much, so the CAC is not high there

- Just like Edtech, for Fintech too the key is awareness. So content marketing would act more efficiently here than spending money on paid ads because people want to understand finance better in simple words for him/her to be able to buy from you.

- Besides, content marketing makes you come across as an expert in your field so if you have won the trust of your customer you have won half the battle.

- Quora and Reddit are excellent channels for projecting yourself as an expert. Go and answer questions on Quora, solve people's problems and see how people are drawn to you and your brand. You have zero CAC there unless of course you want to go for paid ads on Quora – this would have a less CAC than other channels and much more effective since you are being seen as an expert already since you are answering questions there

Is Digital Marketing even effective for B2C businesses? Coz brand building cannot be done via digital media alone

- Brand building is one aspect of the entire Digital Marketing process.

- What channel we use for Brand Building would depend on the product we are selling. For e.g. if I am selling an online course I may not want to build a brand offline for it. So, there are cases where brand building would be done only online via digital media.

- Whether Digital Marketing is effective for a B2C business – Yes, without an iota of doubt! Your reach on FB, Twitter which is the haven for B2C Digital marketing – is way beyond any other channel.

- Again content marketing is the king of all methods. Strong content pulls traffic on social media, boosts SEO.

Is Digital Marketing more effective for B2B business? Is it really worth all the money being charged these days?

- LinkedIn is the most effective channel for B2B. Having a FB ad for your B2B would be burning money. But having a LinkedIn ad for B2B would be a very effective medium.

- Referrals and Word-Of-Mouth play a very big role in B2B marketing because companies need testimonials and references from someone else who has bought from you since the stakes are high. So getting referrals is key here. These strategies cost nothing but play a very big role in B2B marketing

- Content wise case studies would really help. Even boosting a post which has a case study on LinkedIn would be a safe bet.

- So ultimately it is how intelligently you spend the money – what you spend it on and where you spend it.

Best resources to understand digital marketing

- I have always followed Neil Patel (www.neilpatel.com) very closely. I subscribe to the notifications (he almost publishes one article daily). I make it a point to read that article

- To get in-depth knowledge you can also take courses on Udemy. Following is a list of courses that I bought:
    - Mobile App Marketing
    - Complete Social Media Marketing
    - Twitter Marketing
    - Facebook Marketing
    - Youtube Marketing
    - Complete SEO
    - Lead Generation Strategies
    - Google Adwords for Beginners
    - Google Analytics for Beginners
    - Marketing Automation
    - Copywriting

- There is a plethora of information out there. Just narrow down on one subscription which you relate to best and buy short courses (https://thegreycells.com/wordpress-cms/product-category/startup-workshops/) (2-3 days max). The best way to learn is to apply the concepts to your business.

- You might want to read 13 Effective Marketing Tips for Small Businesses (https://expresstext.net/blog/marketing-for-small-business/) for a quick overview of what it takes to get your message out there.

Are automated comments/messages a good idea?

- Automation is the best thing that happened to the Digital Marketing industry!

- Very recently I created a workflow in GetResponse for an Online course. The fact that you can judge the user's intent by the fact that he/she has read your message or not and accordingly take different actions is no less than an instance of Artificial Intelligence in Digital Marketing

- So, yes, automated messages are a good idea.

- Automated comments – it all depends on how intelligently you set up the automation.

- In the same context, chatbots which are automated chats are also recommended no matter what you are selling

- Having said all of this, automation should be complemented by human intervention at the end of the chain. E.g. When we built a chatbot Minty for wealth advisory, we knew that we could only build automation in it upto an extent. At the end of the day, I would not take a financial decision on the basis of what a chatbot tells me. I need a human at the other end to verify the plan.

- So, bottomline, using automated messages/comments/chat is needed, but only at the top end of the funnel. Complement it effectively by closing the deal with human intervention

We find it difficult to generate good sales via ad campaigns …what should be a justifiable budget for digital marketing …or rather budget for Facebook advertisement and Instagram advertisement separately ?

- First and foremost, I would not be right if I would say that X amount is a justifiable budget for Digital Marketing. It depends on a lot of factors which vary widely across businesses

- It depends on

  - The product you are selling. For e.g. if I am selling insurance I better be ready with a huge budget because it is a highly competitive product and there are large players in the market already.

  - Affordability – Obviously, if your business cannot afford it, no matter the requirement, you will not be able to budget that much. But it also goes the other way round. I have seen businesses where people come into a lot of funding all of a sudden and they spend without careful strategising and ending up with a negative ROI. That is the other end of the spectrum which is more scary than not being able to spend at all

  - Quality of the ad campaign – There are ad campaigns that have the capacity to go viral and then there are those which do not generate even a single click. So if you are spending on ads it is important that whosoever is doing it for you knows the tweaks that make an ad sell. Formal education in paid marketing is a must so that whatever budget you have allocated generates a ROI for you.

- Each social media channel has its own voice. What would sell on FB may or may not necessarily sell on Instagram. So yes, budgeting for both should be separately done based on historical performances for your product. How much should that budget be really depends on the above and many more factors.

- A tip here would be to find out (if possible) how much your competitors are spending.

- Start off with what you can afford, observe and analyse for 2-3 cycles and then take the best judgement. Give yourself enough leverage for errors and adjustments

- Check out one of the questions above where I have listed Zero Cost Marketing Techniques and see if they help you minimise your costs

How effective is Facebook Marketing for small businesses with big players spending so much more on this platform as compared to small startups?

- Let me put up some statistics here – 96% of all B2C marketers use social media posts for content marketing. Out of those 97% use Facebook. If everyone is using it, it must be working right?

- There are some aspects of Facebook marketing that we need to consider and keep in mind to succeed at it

  - FB is not a place for cold selling or direct pitching. It is a social media channel. "Social Media" is built on relationships. It is important to understand the Content Marketing Funnel. Start with a lead magnet – a resource that your customer will be interested in, give it away for free. Yes, post an ad for it for a small budget. You may not get a direct sale out of the ad, but someone who is genuinely interested in the resource will click on your ad. That is the beginning of the relationship. An FB ad alone can give a sale but a better bet should be placed on a content marketing funnel, where you attract using FB marketing and then nurture the lead.

- Even big businesses spending a lot of money sometimes lose money on FB Ads if they try to directly pitch.

- Have a complete strategy in place. Its not about creating ads and pushing them, you should know exactly where you are starting and how you will get this customer to buy from you.

- Build an ad, post it, measure its results and optimise. Continue this cycle with a lot of A/B Tests

- Invest time. Spending a designated hour on FB marketing will not help. Monitor and improvise continuously – whatever money you can spend as a small startup will give you effective results if you give it enough time.

- Bottomline, it is not about how much you can spend. FB marketing could be just one part of your entire content marketing cycle. So, aim on completing the entire customer journey and I'm sure FB Ads will play their role wherever they fall in the journey.

- Having said that, keep your mind open to the fact that there maybe some leakage in terms of irrelevant leads and consecutive loss of money there, but that is to be considered as the buffer in your strategy.

Chapter 12

Step 6 - Identifying the Right Team

There is a very popular quote - "It's mostly about people, not strategy".

Well, I beg to differ on that and say that strategy is important. But having said that, yes, I have to admit it is the kind of people that have a bigger role to play. It is these people who have to adopt the strategies that you craft.

It is these people whom you will go on to refer to as your team who have to be completely in harmony with you, your brand, your idea and your company. So a lot of careful thought needs to be given as to what kind of a team you want to create.

Agenda

- Finding your Co-Founder
- Do-It-Yourself or Outsource?
- Best Practices to get the Right Team on board
- Company Culture
- Standard Operating Processes (SOPs)
- ESOPs (Employee Stock Options)

Finding your Co-Founder

As a founder , it tends to get really lonely sometimes. Been there, done that :-)

Having someone to brainstorm each aspect of your startup not only opens the doors of your mind, but also gives you the much needed "another perspective". It is not mandatory to have a co-founder, but definitely recommended.

Here are some things to keep in mind when you are looking for a co-founder.

Complementary Skill Set

Make sure that your prospective co-founder has skill sets which are complementary to yours so that you both can take care of various aspects of your startup in a holistic manner. The perfect combination is a non-techie and a techie co-founder.

Document Commercial Aspects

Make sure there are clear agreements about Profit Sharing, Equity Stake and other money related aspects of getting into such a partnership. Keep everything in black and white.

Define KRAs (Key Result Areas) at the onset

Each of you should have defined activities towards the common goals and takes care of their own domain and gives their best towards the overall growth of the startup.

Define Culture and SOPs (Standard Operating Processes) jointly

More about Culture and SOPs later.

Even though each of you is taking care of their own responsibilities, the company has to have a common ground where both of you agree on the smallest aspects like whether employees will have options to work from home or not, what would be the dress code and so on.

Where to look for your co-founder

- Tap your personal network

- Social Media

- Networking Events

- Sites like http://startupweekend.org/, http://www.startupagents.com/, https://www.cofounderslab.com/. There are many other such founder dating sites

Do-It-Yourself or Outsource?

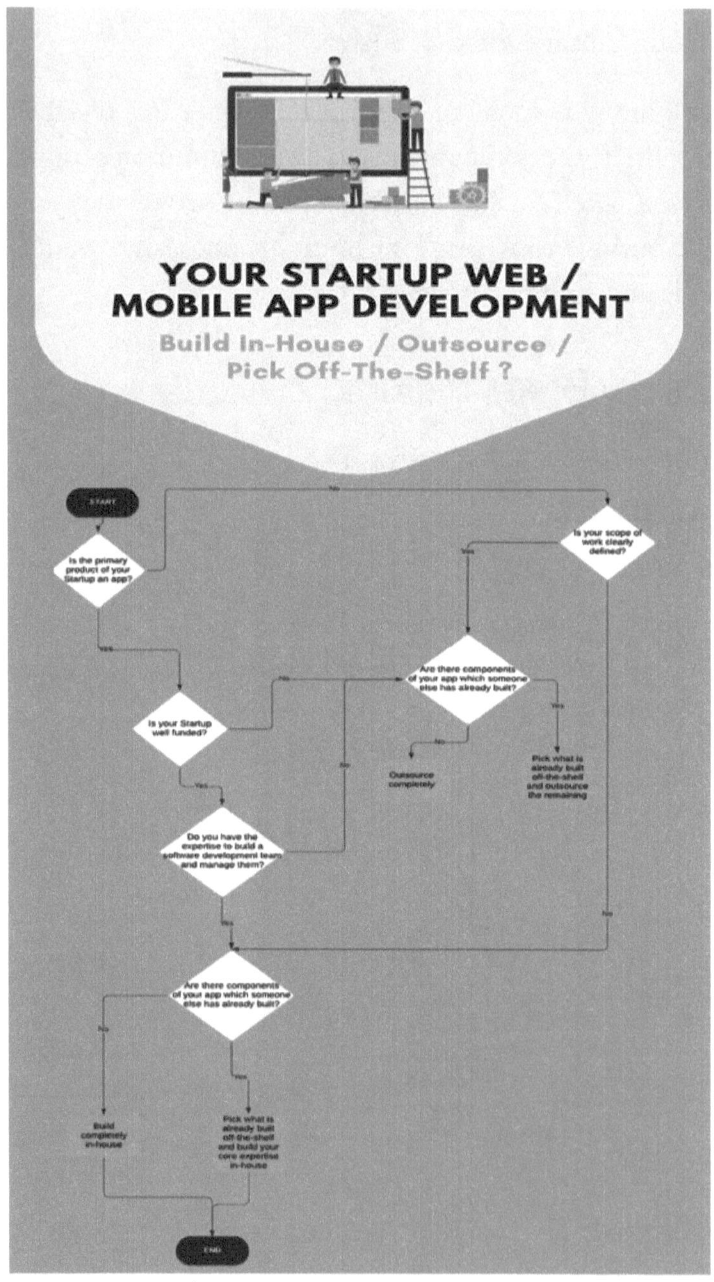

Pros and Cons of In-House

PROS	CONS
Complete Control over Team	Learning Curve
Flexibility and Agility	Recurring Salary and Infra Cost
Intellectual Property Advantage	Focus shifts from core activities

Pros and Cons of Outsource

PROS	CONS
Focus on core activities	Costs can get out of hand sometimes if scope not managed well
No recurring salary and infra cost	Fear of Intellectual Property Leakage
Flexibility to adjust initiatives as per fund availability	External team dependency (not connected with vision)

What can be outsourced

- Software Development
- Quality Assurance (Testing)
- Maintenance

- Content Writing

- Graphics/Creatives

- Social Media Marketing

- Search Engine Optimisation (SEO)

- Paid Marketing

Outsourcing models

	Work Scope	Budget	Technologies Stack	Time Frames	Dedicated Resources	Payment	Team Scalability
FIXED COST MODEL	Predefined	Predefined	Pre-Planned	Predefined	Assigned	Prepayment	Low
DEDICATED RESOURCE HIRING MODEL	Estimated	Gradual	Not Restricted	Estimated	Scalable	Fixed Price for Each Resource per Month	Middle
HOURLY/TIME & MATERIAL MODEL	Not Set	Gradual	Situational	Incremental or Intermittent	Not Assigned	Fixed Price per Hour	High

Best Practices to get the Right Team on board

- In-House HR Team

  - I know that this involves a cost but then having at least one HR professional will help you focus on core activities as the founder rather than spending time on manual hiring processes.

- Accurate Job Descriptions

- Automate manual recruitment processes. Spend time on networking on social media with prospective candidates instead.

  - Job Posting

  - CV Selection based on Keywords

- Shortlisting (Based on written tests)

- Interview Scheduling

- Assessment and Final Selection

- Automate Onboarding and Joining Formalities

- Automation Tools/HRTech Companies

  - Zoho Recruit

  - www.apnahr.in

Company Culture

"Culture" – a very misunderstood term in various aspects. Before I define it in my own way, here are some popular definitions of culture by some of the the most respected dignitaries :

Starbucks was founded around the experience and the environment of their stores. Starbucks was about a space with comfortable chairs, lots of power outlets, tables and desks at which we could work and the option to spend as much time in their stores as we wanted without any pressure to buy. The coffee was incidental.

Until I came to IBM, I probably would have told you that culture was just one among several important elements in any organisation's makeup and success — along with vision, strategy, marketing, financials, and the like... I came to see, in my time at IBM, that culture isn't just one aspect of the game, it is the game. In the end, an organization is nothing more than the collective capacity of its people to create value.

Some worthy points to note in the above 2 quotes :

"The coffee was incidental". The product – Coffee – which served filling in the revenue bank at Starbucks – WAS INCIDENTAL! What was intentional was chairs, tables, a place to talk about work, life without the pressure to buy.

"In the end an organisation is nothing more than the collective capacity of its people to create value". Vision, strategy, financials – all are secondary. It is the people which hone the core of the organisation with is the CULTURE. And one very important point to note here is "collective capacity of people".

What is Startup Culture anyway?

Is it people? Is it the Vision Mission as defined by the CEO probably?

According to me the answer is a BIG NO.

What is the key to a successful startup culture then?

No one can define culture for an organisation. It is inherent. It is crafted over time by the people who make up the organisation. It is an internal code of conduct which is not defined in any HR document. It is an internal code of conduct that the entire team develops over time based on the way they interact with each other to achieve the Vision and the Mission defined by the CEO.

So, yes, having said that it is inherent, it is upon the CEO and Leaders to ensure that what is emerging as the culture of their Startup or any organisation for that matter – is emerging up in the right direction. If not it is their onus and responsibility to keep tweaking it subtly by constant mentoring and coaching. The goal, the vision and the mission is important, no doubt about that. But a healthy organisational culture will boost the push towards the common goal automatically and smoothly.

And mind you, it takes decades sometimes to develop that culture and just a few days sometimes for an untoward incident to wipe it out or change it completely. It is then that the CEO or Leaders need to come in and set it right to what it was.

Why is everyone talking about Culture?

MILL VALLEY, Calif. (July 10, 2019) — Glassdoor, one of the world's largest job and recruiting sites, released a new survey measuring sentiment around mission and culture in the workplace today, along with the level of importance of both. Glassdoor surveyed more than 5,000 adults across four countries: the United States (U.S.), United Kingdom (UK), France and Germany. Among key findings, Glassdoor found that more than three-quarters (77 percent) of adults(1) would consider a company's culture before applying for a job there, and well over half (56 percent) say company culture is more important than salary when it comes to job satisfaction.

The fact that professionals visit Glassdoor at least once to find out about the company proves this fact even more. The fact that companies are now trying really hard to ensure that employees give them a good review on Glassdoor proves that.

Employee productivity and motivation is directly related to culture. Only a happy employee can give optimum productivity. And the best way to manage employee EQ (Emotional Quotient) is to give them a culture where they are not just satisfied but charged up to give up their best.

What is that "happy" culture? Different for every company. It is the people in the company who work together as a team to achieve their goals with a positive mindset. However it may be. Bottomline is achievement of goals with happiness in the mind.

Imbibe a good organisational culture – Subtly

Hire the Right Team

A Right Team is a team with the Right Attitude. As simple as that. Whether they have the skills or not, whether they have the experience or not, the first thing that you should look out for according to me is Attitude.

Skills can be developed with training. Experience comes along the way. Some attain maturity earlier than others. But if the attitude is a problem then no matter the skills or the experience, neither can the employee himself/herself be happy, nor will they be able to deliver what they are expected to deliver.

Appoint the Right Leaders

There are cases where leaders are "appointed". And then there are cases where certain employees are pushed into leadership roles because the situation demands it. Have seen the latter especially in Startups.

Who is a "Right" leader? A person who has the attitude to HELP. Who has the power and the aggressiveness to remove the roadblocks from the way so that his/her team can achieve the milestones and the final goals.

Somehow there is a misconception that leader = boss. Yeah, maybe in some sense, but being a leader does not mean you have to be "bossy". I relate more to "Servant Leaders". According to Wikipedia – Servant leadership is a leadership philosophy in which the goal of the leader is to serve. This is different from traditional leadership where the leader's main focus is the thriving of their company or organisations.

Lead By Example

As a leader if you don't set an example, the team will never follow what you say. Action speaks louder than words, and action is also followed much more than just preaching about what needs to be done.

Not only actions but even your thoughts as a leader will build the inherent culture of the organisation. So be careful about what you speak and what you do. Unknowingly it will be replicated by your team.

Transparency at all times

There are good times and then there are bad. In case of bad times, if it is something that you can handle yourself discreetly, please do. If it is something that, if hidden, has the potential to become a gossip item for employees, then it is better you be transparent about it.

Approachability

Startups promote and follow an open culture. Not just in terms of having the CEO or leader sit beside you on a bean bag and working. But even in terms of being able to walk up to your CEO or leader and ask if they can discuss something with you or at least let you know a convenient time when they can.

For that matter, having coffee and lunch sessions with employees, sometimes one-on-one, sometimes as a group makes you approachable and that plays a very big role on the employe mindset, knowing that you are just a call away when they need you.

Recognise and Reward, Reprimand where deserved

Recognition for good work is a common practice followed by most Startups now. An award on the work table is a big boost for morale.

At the same time, reprimanding when things are not going as expected is not so bad. Sometimes as leaders we have the fear of doing that, especially with the gems, that they might quit if we reprimand them. But done in the right way, it ensures that everyone is grounded enough to accept mistakes and rectify them as soon as possible. If he/she doesn't take it in the right spirit then you are better off without them.

Re-evaluate Your Culture on a regular basis

As a Startup Founder/CEO/Leader, whatever you may call yourself, it is upon you and you only to sit back and observe all the time to see that your company culture is what you want it to be. Be observant enough to see the diversions, smart enough to evaluate them and strong enough to change them if they are not what you want them to be, open enough to incorporate the new good things.

Keep these at bay, no matter what

- Weak communication – Internal and External
- Unhealthy competition
- Gossip
- Working in Silos

Encourage…

- Innovation
- Internal Entrepreneurship
- We Time/Me Time for Employees
- Learning

Last but not the least – Don't forget how you were before you scaled

I have often seen Startup Founders and those who were there with them since inception sit across a coffee and reminisce how things were when they started off. Don't lose those roots. Discuss those roots with new employees too. Tell them those stories. Relive those stories sometimes because they are precious. Cherish them and imbibe some of those habits back again because those were the times that made you who you are today

How a Startup Culture is different

What i am stating below may not be true for all Startups, but is more of my observation in Startups that I have worked with.

- **There are less hierarchical structures in a Startup.** Startups have flat organisational structures. That is probably more of a reason why a single person wears multiple hats. In some ways, that is good but also detrimental to quality. An effective balance needs to be maintained there.

- **A Startup job is not a 9-5 job.** No one forces anyone to stay beyond work hours. It is just the passion sometimes and sometimes it is just because you cant do anything about it anyway. Resources are limited, deadlines are stringent, dreams are BIG. You just have to make it happen by hook or by crook

- This may not be a universal truth but this is just based on my observation. Startups were more open to concepts like remote working, flexible hours even before the pandemic. So **flexibility of working is a notch higher in Startups than large established organisations. The bottomline is getting the job done well and in time, wherever you do it.**

- **Open office culture where anyone sits anywhere**, people are found lounging around with their laptops on bean bags started with startups and large organisations started adopting them down the line.

- In early stage startups especially, people are more committed because they are closely connected to the vision, to the leaders who have created the vision.

Some really cool Startup Culture Habits

- Zappos Founder and CEO Tony Hsieh offers 2000$ for anyone who wants to quit right away. What he is doing is testing how loyal you are to the organisation!

- For every pair of eye glasses that they sell, Warby Parker, gives out a pair to someone really in need.

- Southwest Airlines gives its employees an open permission to take decisions and do whatever they think is right to make the employee happy.

- A lesser known company MindTickle does a Weekly Chaupal – where everyone knows exactly how much revenue came into the company in that week

- Shift Freight, a lesser known company, has taken the initiative to hire those who have lost their jobs during the pandemic

- Cure.Fit has a very bold culture aspect. They don't have a leave policy. They are ok with employees taking a leave anytime provide they are completing their assigned work with quality and on time.

- Once co-founder of Dropbox, Ferdowsi told Jon Ying (an employee) that he didn't want Dropbox's "404 error" page to be so boring. "I remember you like to draw," he told Ying. So Ferdowsi bought some colored pencils and Ying drew up "Psychobox ". Ferdowsi's next statement was, "If you know how to draw, you can do Web design." There Ying started doing Dropbox website design work even though that's not what he used to do earlier.

- Twilio insists that each of its employees must learn to code. If you don't know how to code, Twilio engineers will teach you.

- Evernote has an Officer Training program where employees attend up to two extra meetings a week, in departments they don't work in.

Hope I could set the tone for what Startup Culture is and what it shouldn't be.

Standard Operating Processes (SOPs)

The requirement for defining Standard Operating Processes across the organisation is often underestimated and ignored. Most Startups realise the need and carry out the implementation late in the journey when they realise things are getting messed up and each person in the organisation is doing their own thing. Politics, confusion and clashes arise due to the absence of defined SOPs which must be documented and handed over to each employee on joining. In fact it should be the duty of the HR Team to make sure these policies are being abided on.

Some common SOPs to be drafted :

- HR Policies

- Inter Departmental Communication Policies

- Task Management Tool (and other tools to be used for various purposes)

- Company Intranet

- Customer Relationship Management (CRM) System

- Enterprise Resource Planning (ERP) System (for Accounts, Admin, HR and Operations)

ESOPs (Employee Stock Options)

Employee Stock Options are a benefit offered to most Startup employees these days. The idea is to give a piece of the company to the employee.

How does it work?

- TechStart, hires employee Amit.

- As part of his employment package, TechStart grants Amit options to acquire 40,000 shares of TechStart's common stock at 25 cents per share (the fair market value of a share of TechStart common stock at the time of grant).

- The options are subject to a four-year vesting with one year cliff vesting, which means that Amit has to stay employed with TechStart for one year before he gets the right to exercise 10,000 of the options and then he vests the remaining 30,000 options at the rate of 1/36 a month over the next 36 months of employment.

- If Amit leaves TechStart or is fired before the end of his first year, he doesn't get any of the options.

- After his options are "vested" (become exercisable), he has the option to buy the stock at 25 cents per share, even if the share value has gone up dramatically.

- After four years, all 40,000 of his option shares are vested if he has continued to work for TechStart.

- TechStart becomes successful and goes public. Its stock trades at $20 per share.

- Amit exercises his options and buys 40,000 shares for $10,000 (40,000 x 25 cents).

- Amit turns around and sells all 40,000 shares for $800,000 (40,000 x the $20 per share publicly traded price), making a nice profit of $790,000.

Advantages and Disadvantages

For an employee of course Stock Options give the benefit of the possibility of making a lot of money if the company is successful and its IPO (Initial Public Offering) rocks the share market.

However, if the company doesn't do so, the stock options are not worth anything.

For the company, the biggest advantage is that the employee can be convinced to come in at a lower in-hand salary and more stock options. This ensures loyalty to the company since the company's growth is the employee's growth. Also, prevents attrition since the employee is tied down to the company for a given period of time to be eligible to avail stock options.

The primary disadvantage of Stock Option Plans for the company is the possible dilution of other shareholders' equity when the employees exercise the stock options.

Workshop

CULTURE , SOPs (STANDARD OPERATING PROCESSES)

Document the culture and SOPs for your Startup using this template

https://links.thegreycells.com/CultureSOP

COMPANY HIERARCHY STRUCTURE

Draw a hierarchy structure for your Startup in the form of the Tree Diagram using this template

https://links.thegreycells.com/OrgHierarchy

Templates

- https://links.thegreycells.com/CultureSOP
- https://links.thegreycells.com/OrgHierarchy

Chapter 13

Step 7 - Fundraising

Most of the Startup Founders that I have coached/consulted till now have given me a dazed and confused look when I have asked them "How much Funding do you need?".

And come to think of it at the beginning of their association, when I asked them what was their biggest challenge they said "Bas Funding ka karwa do Ma'am, baaki sab ho jaayega (Just get us the Funding somehow Ma'am, the rest will be taken care of)"

And I completely understand the sentiment behind this challenge. Especially, as a non-finance person myself, **I understand that playing around with numbers is a pain. However, when I actually went to do it, I realised it involves just 2 skills – logic and simple arithmetic.**

So much so, that I put all my workings into a Google Sheet and created a Startup **Business Financials Template** at the request of many Startup Founders, so that they could just key in their numbers and get an idea about projected Expenses, Revenue and PnL Statements. Powered with that information and the money that they can use for Self Funding their Startup , they would have an idea of exactly how much Funding is needed, based on the deficit.

For that matter, even if you are going on the self-funded path this can help you align your finances with your goals.

Disclaimer : You will still need a Finance Expert to work this out with you. This is just from the Knowledge Point of View

Agenda :

- Assessing the Addressable Market Size

- How much Funding do you need?

- Estimating Valuation

- Term Sheet

- Fundraising Levels and knowing what applies to you

- Where to find investors?

- Finding the right investor match

- Negotiation with Investors

- Crafting the Investor Pitch Deck

Assessing the Addressable Market Size

Getting a reasonably accurate and realistic estimate of your projected revenue and hence consequent valuation of your Startup is going to be the deciding factor for an investor to take a call on whether he/ she should put money into your Startup.

At the end of the day, what returns an investor reaps from the investment they make and as the Startup Founder it is your responsibility to present these projections as scientifically as possible.

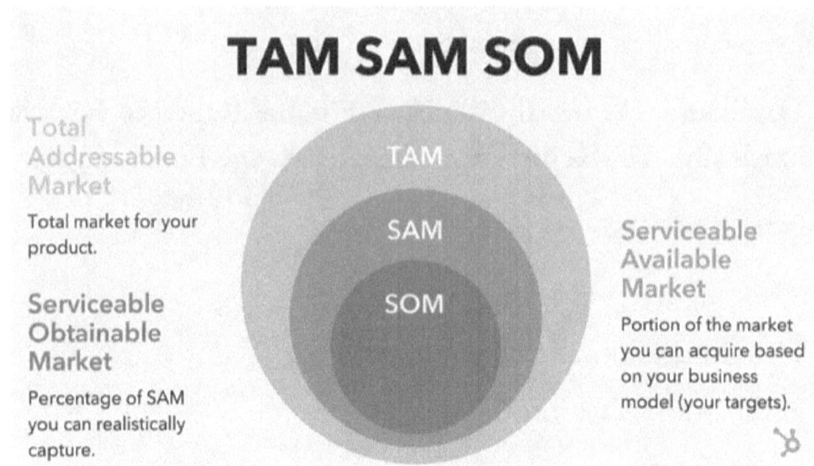

Image Ref : Hubspot

TAM, SAM and SOM are the 3 parameters which will give you an assessment about the market size.

Example : Fast Food Chain

TAM : Worldwide Fast Food Consumers

SAM : Fast Food Consumers in the City you are staying in

SOM : A given percentage of Fast Food Consumers in the City you are staying in after you factor in the competition

Let's say you are starting a fast food chain. Your TAM would be the worldwide fast food restaurant market. Potentially, if you were present in every country and had no competition you would generate TAM as revenues.

Sorry but that's not going to happen!

Let's be more realistic. You are starting your restaurant chain in two cities where the demand for fast food can be estimated based on: the population, their food habits, and the revenues generated by fast food restaurants in other cities having similar demographics.

That is your Serviceable Available Market: the demand for you type of products within your reach. In other words if you were the only fast food in town you would generate revenues of SAM.

Now you are probably not the only fast food in town...

So realistically you can hope to capture only a fraction of your SAM. Most likely you will attract fast food aficionados living or working close to your restaurants and a fraction of the people located further away that are willing to give your chain a try for the sake of fast food diversity. This is your SOM.

Significance of TAM, SAM, SOM for the Investor

- SOM is the short term target proves that you are capable of delivering your promise and is the first level de-risking assurance
- SAM is the long term target which shows that you can scale
- TAM is the holistic potential of your business which will encourage the investor to keep investing.

How much Funding do you need?

Projected Revenue Calculations

You would have done the Product Pricing activity in the Step 5 - Marketing, Sales and Post-Sales session. Knowing the pricing of each product/service and the SOM, these 2 factors when multiplied should be good enough for you to estimate the Projected Revenues.

https://links.thegreycells.com/BusinessFinancials

Projected Expense Calculations

This is the biggest pain point to arrive at.

Each Startup will have its own Expense Accounts. For a general understanding I am considering 3 main Expense Accounts here.

- Employee Salaries
- Tools
- Marketing Costs

Employee Salaries Expenses

Before even deciding Employee Salaries, you need to work out the Team Structure carefully. Keep in mind, that this gets a little out of hand because as a Startup Founder you want to achieve everything in as less time as possible. Be a little frugal here and consider team members which you need as a bare minimum.

Tools Expenses

I am a firm believer in the concept of Automation.

Automate as much as you can since as a Startup Founder, there is no end to the things that you have to manage. Having said that, it doesn't mean that you have to lose complete control over your Work-Life Balance. (Another post on that coming soon). Subscribing to some basic tools like Asana for Task Management, Zoho for Marketing, CRM , Canva for Social Media Post creation and many more like that which you can check out in this article "How to run your Startup in Robot Mode"

Yes, there is a cost involved, but think about the time and energy that you save when you delegate half your work to an Automation

Tool. As a Startup Founder, time is money for you, so don't be frugal on this expense.

Marketing Expenses

This calculation is a little complex, but finally based on logic and simple arithmetic.

"Paid is Freedom", I have often heard. So Paid Marketing is the holy grail of all your expenses and will form the biggest chunk of your Expense Sheet.

It all starts with CPC (Cost Per Click) which is the money that you pay for each click on your Ad in any of the Paid Marketing networks like Google or Facebook. For a Startup Founder, who was just ignited by an Idea and the passion to take it to heights, all this becomes kind of a drudgery. But, there is no way out of it, so you better spend time on understanding this.

So, say based on industry averages you discovered that the average CPC for your product P1 is Rs. 5. Hold these figures in your mind and we will come back to them.

Say, your SOM is 500 customers.

Now suppose you decide to execute some Facebook ads to get these 500 paying customers. People will see your ads, this is the Traffic that comes for your ads. If your ad is interesting enough, they will click on your ad. Facebook charges you money for this click. This is CPC (the amount that you pay for each click). Once they click the ad, they will go to your landing page. They find it interesting and they provide their email id and/or phone number on your landing page. Here you got a Lead. Your marketing is over, now sales begin. I would recommend Nurturing Automation to close the sale with a final call in the end. If you are good at it, the Lead becomes a Paying Customer.

Say, from whatever Traffic comes to your ads, 5% click on your ad. This is the Traffic to Click conversion ratio, also popularly called CTR (Click Through Rate).

Now, let's take some general assumptions that we need to know to do the further calculations. These assumptions may vary depending on industry, quality of ad and many other factors. For example, here is an idea about CTR (click through rate for industry)

Say, 10% get converted to Leads. This is also called Click-To-Lead Conversion Ratio. Also from whatever Leads come through your Landing page, say, 2% get converted to Customers. This is also called Lead-To-Customer Ratio.

We are going to go reverse here now.

For achieving the target of 500 paying customers and considering Lead-To-Customer Ratio of 2% you will need to do the following calculations :

Paying Customers Target = 500

Lead-To-Customer Ratio = 2%

Leads = 500/2% = 25000

For achieving the target of 25000 Leads and considering Click-To-Lead Ratio of 10% you will need to do the following calculations :

Leads = 25000

Click-To-Lead Ratio = 10%

Clicks needed = 25000/10% = 250000

You had arrived at a CPC (Cost Per Click) of Rs. 5 per click above. So, here you have your paid marketing expense calculated as follows :

Clicks needed = 2,50,000

CPC (Cost Per Click) = Rs. 5

Marketing Budget needed = 250000 * 5 = 12,50,000

There will be some miscellaneous marketing costs like Email, SMS costs for organic marketing. There will also be website hosting costs. Like I said earlier, each Startup will have some additional costs over and above the basic costs discussed which they cannot do without.

So, your total Projected Expenses will be as follows :

Project Expenses = Employee Salaries + Tools + Marketing Expenses

Final Figure – How much Funding do you need

Finally we are at a point where we can arrive at the golden figure – How much Funding do you need?

Well, tap your self funding resources to see how much you can arrange from your kitty. The deficit between that and the Projected Expenses you arrived at above is the figure for the Funding you need.

Estimating Valuation

Startup valuations provide insight into a company's ability to

- **use invested capital to grow**

- **meet customer and investor expectations**

- **Scale to hit the next milestone**

If you have actual revenues, you're able to use concrete economic numbers as a starting point. But in the context of fundraising, your company is ultimately worth what you and your investors agree it's worth. And most angel investors and venture capital firms use multiple formulas to find the pre-money value of a business, or how much it's worth before they invest.

Groundwork needed

- Projected Balance Sheet (which you have prepared above)

- Industry Databases like Angelist and Crunchbase for market comparison

Factors affecting Valuation

There are factors to be considered when making the valuation of a company, with the main ones listed below:

- Traction – Does the target startup have customers?

- Prototype – A Proof Of Concept (PoC), makes a positive impression on investors.

- Present Funding – Indicates a business owner's desperation to secure an investment

- Existing Revenues – Existing recurring payments from clients, the more robust the valuation will be.

- Reputation – Does the founder or his team have a track record of good ideas and executing them up to market adoption phase? Does the product already have a good reputation? A startup is more likely to obtain a higher valuation with those particularities, even when there isn't any traction yet.

- Current Status of Sector – In case the target company belongs to a booming or popular (like mobile gaming or fintech) industry investors are more likely to pay a premium when buying equity.

- Management Team Capability - Credentials and Experience of Core Team Members , their financial planning capabilities.

- Saturated Market - Red Ocean

- Product Quality - Reviews and Ratings Assessment of product

- Profit Margins allocation

  How to determine pre-money value of a business

The Berkus Method

The Berkus Method was created by venture capitalist Dave Berkus to find valuations specifically for pre-revenue startups, i.e., businesses not yet selling their products at scale. The idea is to assign dollar amounts to five key success metrics found in early-stage startups.

If it exists:	Add to company value (up to):
Sound Idea (basic value)	$500,000
Prototype (reducing technology risk)	$500,000
Quality Management Team (reducing execution risk)	$500,000
Strategic relationships (reducing market risk)	$500,000
Product Rollout or Sales (reducing production risk)	$500,000

This method caps pre-revenue valuations at $2 million and post-revenue valuations at $2.5 million. This is the simplest way of arriving at your Startup Valuations.

Comparable Transactions Method

The Comparable Transactions Method is one the most popular startup valuation techniques. You're answering the question, "How much were startups like mine acquired for?"

For instance, imagine that Tomato, a fictional foodtech startup, was acquired for $24 million. Its mobile app and website had 700,000 users. That's roughly $34 per user. Your foodtech startup has 120,000 users. That gives your business a valuation of about $4 million.

Market Multiples Approach

You can also find revenue multiples for similar companies in your sector. In your market, it may be normal for SaaS companies to generate 5x to 7x the previous year's net revenue.

You can take that as a benchmark however, this does not necessarily mean that you will also achieve the same. You have to factor in year of business, Intellectual Property Status and many other factors. Accordingly you may raise or lower the multiple.

Scorecard Valuation Method

The Scorecard Method is another option for pre-revenue businesses. It also works by comparing your startup to others that are already funded but with added criteria.

First, you find the average pre-money valuation of comparable companies. Then, you'll consider how your business stacks up according to the following qualities.

Step #1 Finding The Average Industry Pre-Money Valuation

Average:	US$ 1.67 million
Mode:	US$ 1.50 million
Low:	US$ 1.00 million
High:	US$ 2.70 million

Step #2 Determining The Individual Weighted Averages and assign Comparison Factors to arrive at a sum of factors

COMPARISON FACTOR	WEIGHT %	COMPARISON %	FACTOR = (WxC)
Strength of Entrepreneur and Team	30%	100%	0.3000
Size of the Opportunity	25%	125%	0.3125
Product/Technology	15%	150%	0.2250
Competitive Environment	10%	80%	0.0800
Marketing/Sales/Partnerships	10%	100%	0.1000
Need for Additional Investment	5%	100%	0.0500
Other factors (great location)	5%	125%	0.0625
SUM			1.1300

Step #3 Multiplying The Sum Of The Factors

For the final step, we multiply the sum of the factors, 1.1300, by the average industry pre-money valuation in step one, US$1.5 million, to get our own company pre-money valuation. Here, we have a pre-money valuation of US$1.7 million dollars!

$1.5M * 1.13 = $1.7M

Cost-to-Duplicate Approach

The key to this method is in the name. You're figuring out how much it would cost to recreate your startup elsewhere — minus any intangible assets, like your brand or goodwill.

You simply add up the fair market value of your physical assets. You may also include research and development costs, product prototype costs, patent costs, and more.

One major drawback is that this method inherently doesn't capture the full value of a company, particularly if it's generating revenue. In calculating your startup's valuation, you may have to ignore elements that are particularly relevant, like your customer engagement.

Risk Factor Summation Method

This is a broader method of valuing your startup. Start with an initial valuation based on one of the other methods mentioned here. Then, increase or decrease that monetary value in multiples of $250,000 based on risks affecting your business.

Low-risk elements get a double-plus grade (++), which means you add $500,000 to your valuation. High-risk elements get a double-minus grade (--), and you subtract $500,000.

For instance, if your online custom clothing store has a slight but low risk of competition, you can grade it positively but add only $250,000.

The 12 common risk categories are as follows:

- Management
- Stage of the business
- Legislation/political risk
- Manufacturing risk
- Sales and marketing risk
- Funding/capital raising risk
- Competition risk
- Technology risk
- Litigation risk
- International risk
- Reputation risk
- Potential lucrative exit

The difficult portion of this method is finding an objective point of reference to measure each component. Starting with comparable methods, like the Scorecard Method or Comparable Transactions Approach, may help.

Venture Capital Method

As the name suggests, this method is a go-to for venture capital firms, and it's another option to consider if you need a pre-revenue valuation. It also reflects the mindset of investors who are looking to exit a business within several years.

It uses the following formulae:

Return on Investment (ROI) = Terminal (or Harvest) Value ÷ Post-money Valuation

Post-money Valuation = Terminal Value ÷ Anticipated ROI

Terminal (or Harvest) value is the startup's targeted anticipated selling price in the future. It is estimated by using reasonable expectation for revenues and earnings in the year it will be sold.

If we have a software business with a terminal value of US$2,000,000 with an anticipated return of investment of 10X and they need US$50,000 to get a positive cash flow we can do the following calculations.

Post-money Valuation = Terminal Value ÷ Anticipated ROI = $2 million ÷ 10X

Post-money Valuation = $200,000

Pre-money Valuation = Post-money Valuation − Investment = $200,000 − $50,000

Pre-money Valuation = $150,000

Term Sheet

A Term Sheet is a non-binding document that outlines the offered terms and conditions under which an investment will be made by an "Angel" or a Venture capital investor.

Disclaimer : This is a technical aspect from the finance point of view and must be prepared with a certified finance executive like a CA.

Example Term Sheet Draft

https://links.thegreycells.com/TermSheetDraft

Fundraising Levels and knowing what applies to you

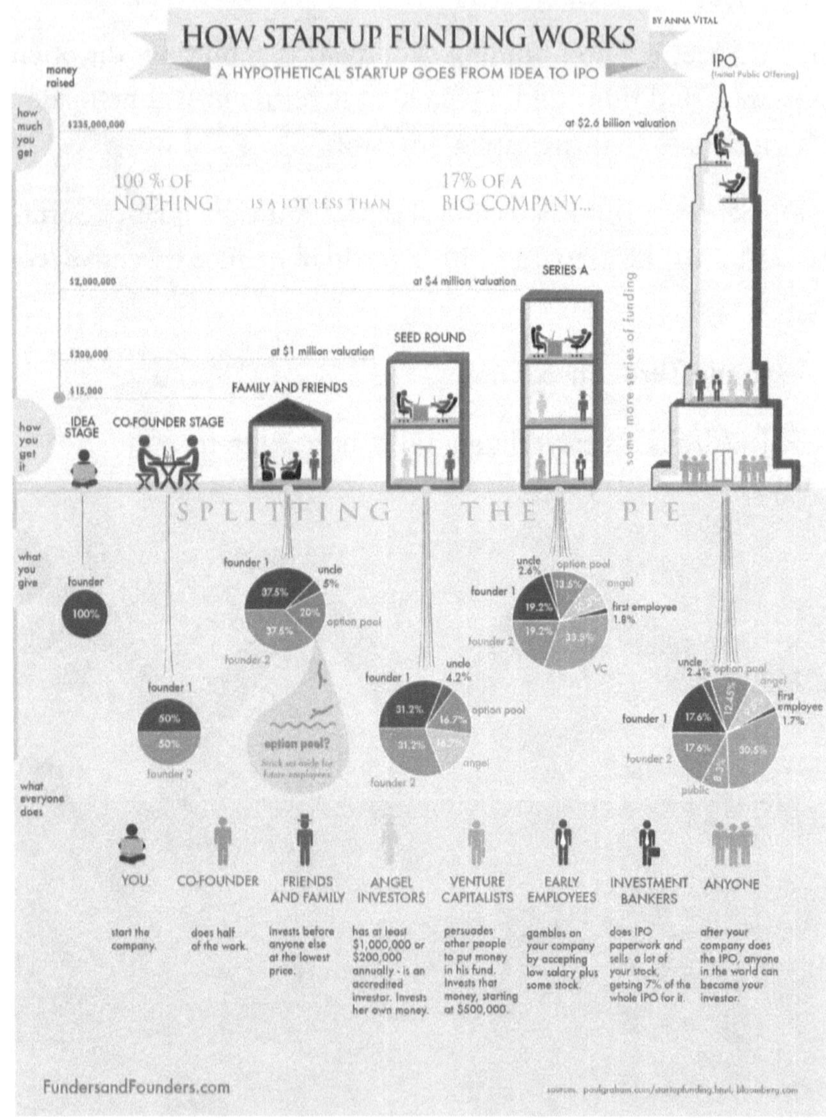

https://thumbnails-visually.netdna-ssl.com/how-startup-funding-works_51db987f390b4_w1500.png

Types of investors

- **Friends and Family**
- **Crowdfunding**
  - opens up the opportunity for investment to literally everyone. By using websites such as Kickstarter, GoFundMe and Indiegogo, you can pitch your business idea or product and let people around the world
- **Angel Investors**
  - Individuals who invest their personal money into your company for a return
- **Incubators/Accelerators**
  - Businesses in the Pre-Seed Stage that show significant promise can apply to incubators or accelerators to receive a number of benefits. In most cases, if your company is invited to participate in one of these programs, you can expect a state-of-the-art work environment, business mentorship, strong industry connections, and for the most promising ventures, seed funding.
- **Venture Capitalists (VCs)**
  - These investors are part of the private sector and have a pool of money to draw from corporations, foundations, pension funds, and organizations.
  - These firms will play a more active role in your startup, as they will receive some equity in exchange for funding, and will help provide expertise in guiding you throughout your development stages.

- **Venture Debt**
  - This type of funding is only available to those entrepreneurs whose company is already venture-backed. Venture debt funding is essentially a loan that you will have to repay, regardless of if the company is profitable, without having to give up any equity.

- **Private Equity**
  - Private equity firms invest in startups or businesses through shares or ownership in the company. A private equity firm usually raises funds for investments through large third-party investors such as universities, charities, pension plans or insurance companies.

- **Bank Loans**

Where to find investors?

Some solid reference links in the References section with directories of incubators, accelerators, angel investors and Venture Capitalists. Roll up your sleeves, hunt them down on linked in and send them messages in the prescribed format and get started on the funding activity for your startup

- Offline Community Meetups
- Online Communities - Groups on social media
- LinkedIn and other Social Media Networking sites
  - Some solid reference links in the References section to advise you on what to write in your outreach message to investors to make sure it resonates with them and inspires them to respond.
- Incubators and Accelerators

- Mutual Contacts
- Networking Events
- Hackathons
- Sites like Crunchbase

Finding the right investor match

When you onboard an investor, that institution or individual becomes part of your cap table, and it's for the long run. So make sure, you take time and choose them wisely.

Sufficient fund availability

- When was the last time the prospective investor funded something?
- How much does the investor have left?
- How are the investor's other investments performing?

To track funds activity you can use websites like CB Insights or Crunchbase.

Specific Domain or Diversified

Check if they fund Startups in your domain. If not, are they open to diversification?

Influence

- How much influence do they have in your industry, with other investors, with distribution and media channels, and with other influencers?
- Do they have the capability to bring more investors on board from their network?

Personal Reputation

- Easy to get along with

- Control Freak?

Industry expertise (Desirable)

What industry does your investment partner come from? It's typically a good idea to find investment partners who understand the ins and outs of your industry, ideally through hands-on experience. These investors should have deep knowledge of how the industry has historically changed over time, the market forces affecting it now, and where it's headed. When your investors are familiar with your industry, they can provide insight and practical advice to address the market and avoid pitfalls.

Functional expertise

Investors with functional expertise have mastery in some or all of the foundational skills associated with entrepreneurship and fundraising. Basically, you want your investors to know what they're doing, so that they can help take your business to the next level.

- If they're angel investors, have they built and/or sold a company?

- Have they acted as advisors to startups in the past, or been founders themselves?

- If they're firms, do they specialise in finance or industry-specific analytics?

- Do they typically help startups with their operational challenges?

Ask other founders about the investors you're talking to, and dig into their backgrounds to uncover the value they can offer you beyond just money.

Track Record

Have they worked with companies that look like yours?

Ideally, you'll look for venture capital firms with a history of successful investments and exits. One way to evaluate a firm's track record is through its gross internal revenue (IRR). Firms with a higher IRR over a longer period of time are theoretically more seasoned and better suited to help you grow your business. Different firms typically set different IRR goals for their portfolios, depending on the stage of companies they routinely invest in. Early-stage investors, for example, typically target a 30% net IRR over eight years, while many late-stage investors set a target net IRR of around 20% over the same period.

Many of the most successful angel investors are former entrepreneurs who built successful startups of their own. You can also seek out references from people who've previously worked with a particular firm to get an idea of how they respond when their investments begin to go south.

Negotiation with Investors

The process of negotiating with investors implies many factors that have to be well managed to achieve the desired outcomes. There is no magic recipe for successful negotiations with potential investors, however and if you want to negotiate like an expert, the following key points will help you to get closer to your goals.

Develop a partnership mindset

When a VC invests money in your startup they are not doing you a favour. Their clear intention is to get 8X-10X returns for their investment.

Treat it as a partnership deal and negotiate for a win-win.

Go with a finance professional

Make sure you walk in for a negotiation with your Chartered Accountant or whosoever is the appointed expert for dealing with money matters.

The point here is not that you don't trust the VC, the point is that if you are not equipped to understand complicated terms in the term sheet, you may delay the chances of getting the funding soon. Having a finance professional on board will help speed up the process when complicated terms like liquidation preference and participation are thrown at you out of the blue.

Avoid Desperation and leverage your advantages

In case you are in a cash burn-out situation while negotiating the deal, pivot the discussion from whether the VC could leverage the start-up's weak position in order to meet short-term goals to whether doing so would actually achieve the VC's ultimate goals.

Identify and leverage sources of power even when you're out of money and seemingly out of options as well. Persuade the VC that forcing you to accept harsh terms could be an imaginary victory, because an equity dilution could cause the start-up to falter or even fail, zeroing out the VC's investment.

Keep the ethics intact

In VC relationships, as in any long-term partnership, it's much easier to build trust than to rebuild it. If you find you've settled on terms without sufficient consideration or have made commitments you cannot keep, you're better off playing it straight

Focus on Value (Not Just Valuation)

Very often, founders of startups are fixated on the percentage of shares they want to keep for themselves. At first glance, it seems normal for every founder that the majority of the shares should stay in his/her control to manage the company.

Would you rather have 25% in Google shares, or 90% shares of a startup that just started 2 months ago?

Crafting the Investor Pitch Deck

You have done all the hard work and created all the artefacts. All you need to do is to put up the core pitch points in a Pitch Deck that says it all.

https://links.thegreycells.com/PitchDeckTemplate

Reference : 30 Legendary Startup Pitch Decks and What You Can Learn From Them (+10 Free Templates)

https://piktochart.com/blog/startup-pitch-decks-what-you-can-learn/

Workshop

Tam Sam Som

Research and arrive at figures for TAM SAM SOM. Present them using this template

https://links.thegreycells.com/TAMSAMSOM

Business Financials

Work out your projected expenses and revenue models and arrive at PnL figures using this template

https://links.thegreycells.com/BusinessFinancials

Investor Pitch Deck

Study investor decks of popular Startups here - https://piktochart. com/blog/startup-pitch-decks-what-you-can-learn/ and present your factuals in an Investor Pitch Deck using this template or any other of your choice

https://links.thegreycells.com/PitchDeckTemplate

Templates

- https://links.thegreycells.com/TAMSAMSOM

- https://links.thegreycells.com/BusinessFinancials

- https://links.thegreycells.com/PitchDeckTemplate

- https://piktochart.com/blog/startup-pitch-decks-what-you-can-learn/

References

- https://links.thegreycells.com/TermSheetDraft
- Cold Pitch on LinkedIn
  - https://www.hatchbuck.com/blog/cold-outreach-templates-linkedin/
  - https://www.slideshare.net/TomMallens/20-successful-linkedin-messages
  - https://neilpatel.com/blog/social-media-cold-outreach/
  - https://business.linkedin.com/en-uk/marketing-solutions/blog/posts/sales-solutions/2019/5-templates-for-sales-emails-and-InMails-that-really-work
  - https://www.linkedin.com/business/sales/blog/management/how-to-personalize-your-inmail-pitch
- Approaching a VC on LinkedIn
  - https://yourstory.com/2017/03/approach-vc-funding-linkedin
  - https://www.linkedin.com/pulse/7-secrets-linkedin-fundraising-your-start-up-andrey-gidaspov/
  - https://www.linkedin.com/pulse/how-find-investors-linkedin-engage-them-properly-jon-stoddard/
  - https://salon.thefamily.co/the-art-of-raising-angel-funds-on-linkedin-94cdd3ce193
  - https://sproutsocial.com/insights/how-to-find-investors-linkedin/
  - https://rflavin.com/blog/finding-investors-startup-linkedin/
  - https://venturesone.com/how-to-approach-a-vc-on-linkedin/

- https://www.entrepreneur.com/article/293888
- https://www.business2community.com/linkedin/build-linkedin-profile-attract-investors-01993551

- Directories for Incubators/Accelerators
  - https://nextbigwhat.com/incubators-and-accelerators-in-india-list/
  - https://incubatorlist.com/
  - https://golden.com/query/list-of-incubator-companies-NMB3

- Directories for Angel Investors
  - https://digest.myhq.in/active-angel-investors-india/
  - https://inc42.com/resources/top-37-angel-investors-india/

- Directories for Venture Capitalists
  - https://inc42.com/resources/top-47-active-venture-capital-firms-india-startups/
  - http://www.primepevcdatabase.com/
  - https://www.crunchbase.com/hub/india-venture-capital-investors
  - https://coffeemug.ai/meet/investors

Chapter 14

Putting It All Together

— ANTOINE DE SAINT-EXUPERY

You woke up one fine morning with an out of the world Startup Idea which could become a booming business.

What next?

Should you rent out a place, hire a team, tell them what you want and set out to meet investors to fund your dream? Ok, let me complicate it more for you. Which one of these should you do first?

Sure, you know that a Business Plan needs to be in place before you start off on your next big venture. But what is a Business Plan anyway? Is it some gibberish that is to be written in a Word Document so that you can claim that you have it when stakeholders ask you about it? Or should it be that this sacrosanct document needs to have not just your dreams, but a clear action plan to achieve those dreams.

Your Startup Business Plan should be an actionable entity. Whenever I have created Business Plans for Startups whom I have consulted I have named it as "Company X Bible". I tell them, this is your Go-To document for everything related to your dream. Your thoughts, your guide, your plan. If you write it and forget about it years later, it really makes no sense spending the time and energy to create it.

Here are the must-have elements without which your Business Plan is incomplete. Well, I would never say a Business Plan is complete anyway. If you don't feel the need to keep revisiting your Business Plan and updating it with new thoughts all the time, then it's time you need to re-evaluate your dreams again.

Make sure you check off each item on this exhaustive checklist before you declare it usable.

Complete Startup Templates Toolkit

Vision

This section should articulate your hopes and dreams for the business.

Mission

The Mission should describe how you intend to achieve your vision. For example:

Products And Services

List and describe each product and/or service your business provides. Focus on your customers' perspective (and needs) by demonstrating the problem you are trying to solve.

Revenue Model

The pricing strategy section needs to demonstrate how your business will be profitable. Summarize your projected revenue and expenses:

Market Research And Analysis

Who your target audience is, where you will find customers, how you will reach them and, most importantly, how you will deliver your product or service to them.

Marketing Plan

This section describes how you intend to get the word out to customers about your services.

https://links.thegreycells.com/ContentCalendarT

Financial Plan

Ensure you enlist an Accountant to create a Cash Flow Statement, Funding Requirements

https://links.thegreycells.com/BusinessFinancialsT

Team Plan

This section should list key members of the management team, the founders/owners, board members, advisors and a detailed Team Hierarchy Diagram.

Product Release Plan

What will be the phases involved with timelines and milestones?

https://links.thegreycells.com/ProductReleasePlanT

Action Plan

Briefly describe the action items needed to achieve your objectives, using milestone dates. For example : By "date," a fully equipped office will be completed.

Chapter 15

Useful Startup Tool Series – Calendly Appointment Scheduling Tool

"Time is what we want most, what we use worst"
— WILLIAM PENN

How many times have you scheduled 2 meetings at the same time on the same day because you were using say iCloud for your work meetings and Google Calendar for your personal meetings.. or worse still not using any calendar at all? Ever felt that you declared yourself available on Monday at 11am but something came up at 10:00am and you had no way to reschedule except send back and forth emails?

As a business owner , the time and energy you save is proportionally equal to the money that you could make in the saved time. Using simple tools can help you get there and maintain your sanity amidst the chaos called entrepreneurship.

Let me introduce you today to an awesome Appointment Scheduling Tool called Calendly. It has helped me save at least 20% of the time I would have otherwise spent scheduling meetings back and forth on emails and increased my prospects because I give them an actionable Call to Action. I am sure it will be a big time and energy saver for you too. So here goes..

https://youtu.be/0PRdu_k6oIA

Chapter 16

Useful Startup Tool Series – Asana Task Management Tool

"For every minute spent organising, an hour is earned"
— BENJAMIN FRANKLIN

What is it about being organised that it is becoming the prime talk of the town? Are only perfectionists supposed to be organised? What does all that effort around being organised give us in return anyway?

Hi, I am Anu Khanchandani – Engineer, Entrepreneur and Business Coach for the past 25 years. And yes, accused of being a perfectionist to the point of nagging people around me to be organised in all aspects of their lives – be it personal or professional.

Let me introduce you today to an awesome Task Management Tool called Asana. It has changed my life over the past 6 years and I am sure it will change yours too. So here goes..

https://youtu.be/g7Wq1TpC_e8

Chapter 17

Startup Idea Directory

"The value of an idea lies in the using of it"
— THOMAS EDISON

As a Startup Coach/Consultant I must have come across more than 500 Startup Ideas.

There are 2 kinds of Startup Founders. Those who clearly know what they want but don't know how to go about getting it done. And then there are those who carry tons of business experience with them but are still thinking about what Startup Idea could be the next big thing.

For the second category of Startup Founders, I have jotted down my entire collection of Startup Ideas (some which came to me while travelling, some while I was on vacation!).

The goal is to solve pain points for the common man. So, if you always had it in you to launch yourself as an entrepreneur, feel free to pick up any thought and start working on it. **If you want me to help you** (https://links.thegreycells.com/startup-coaching), it would be my utmost privilege.

- **Last Minute Revision**

  - This app is designed for students or for that matter for anybody pursuing a course in which you have to give an exam.

  - Last minute revision is a critical exam technique sometimes and ensures that everything is fresh in your mind just before you enter the exam hall. Instead of flipping through pages of your book and trying to frantically find everything that you would like to remember, isn't it better that you have it stored in your mobile in an app

  - https://thegreycells.com/blog/tech-startup-idea-edtech-solution-exam-blues/

- **Online Tuition Marketplace**

  - Why limit students to teachers only from local areas? Why not give a student an opportunity to learn from the best teachers around the world. And vice versa too. Why not give teachers the opportunity to achieve global expertise by giving them an opportunity to teach syllabi all across the world?

  - This is the concept that the Online Tuition Marketplace is based on.

  - https://thegreycells.com/blog/startup-business-idea-online-tuition-marketplace/

- **Interior Design Planner**

  - One of the most tedious activities a couple has to go through is a home shift. Right from a flower vase to a customised closet, their mind is bogged down by the amount of activities I had to manage related to home shifting.

- Why not organise it all for them in an app which helps them manage their budget, look for vendors, visualise interior design before its done and a lot more.

- https://thegreycells.com/blog/startup-idea-interior-design-app/

- **Second Career – Women after a Break**

  - A platform to assist women who have taken a career break due to any reason by providing them the following facilities on an online platform

    - Updating past experience

    - Skill upgradation based on future plan

    - Day care for kids

    - House help

- **Track School Bus**

  - An app with geolocation facilities to track children's school bus and take the worry off parents mind

  - https://thegreycells.com/blog/trackschoolbus-starts-up-a-case-study/

- **Cool Gadget Collection**

  - One of a kind gadget platform with extraordinary gadgets is bich can be of utility and wow the audience

- **Educational Games for children**

  - A complete online platform to teach various concepts via games so that there is a practical implementation of a concept in an enjoyable way

- **Online Exhibitions Marketplace**
  - Online platform for exhibition setup and management
  - Facilities like virtual tour and more to entice exhibition owners to sign up

- **Comprehensive Formulae Collection**
  - Formulae are the crux of many science and math subjects. A complete labelled , searchable encyclopaedia of all kinds of formulae with customisations so that students can focus only on those applicable to them

- **Legal Arbitration Centre**
  - Legal Arbitration has become a popular way of solving legal issues out of court. A complete online platform for legal experts and clients to connect and manage all steps in a legal arbitration scenario

- **Garage Sale**
  - A platform for managing garage sales to connect organisers , customers and shippers on one ground

- **CarPool**
  - An app to allow people in a given location to announce availability or otherwise book a car pool with someone who has offered.

- **Spare Parts**
  - A platform for buy/sell of spare parts of all kinds. This will require comprehensive cataloging to cover all types.

- **Charter Booking**
  - An exclusive app dedicated to booking Charter Flights across Charter Service providers

- **Courier Cargo Booking**
  - A platform to book domestic and international courier and cargo packages with instant availability of rates from various providers and online payments with tracking

- **Nature Enthusiasts**
  - Photography and informative catalog of all places to visit for nature enthusiasts

- **Parenting**
  - Although this is a very popular category where blogs are concerned, this could be extended to provide workshops and day care centres and any facility that could help new parents. Also a professional guide by doctors and psychologists for career counseling and aptitude development for children of various ages.

- **Industry focused Job Sites**
  - This has been a pet project for me. The vision here is to develop a recruitment platform with a common base which can be then extended to any industry and used in a customised manner.

- **Fuel Saver**
  - A device which can be attached to your steering wheel to guide you on how to adjust speed so that you can use less fuel.

- **Housing Society Management**
  - A platform to manage housing society activities. Yes, there are already many platforms like this but you can always add an edge by providing special services related to security and

other important aspects using latest technologies like IoT, Blockchain etc.

- **Hospice Management**

  - A platform dedicated to providing healthcare for elders and others with special needs.

- **Art Marketplace**

  - A platform to allow artists to showcase their talent.

- **Legal Cases Database**

  - A comprehensive searchable database of all court cases documentation which legal professionals can use as a subscription.

- **Startup Social Network**

  - Again, a pet project for me where I visualise to create a community of Startups, which can provide not just a communication platform but also a business service platform where Startups can even barter service between each other instead of spending on outsourcing or recruiting in-house teams

- **Property Agent Co-ordination**

  - The real estate listing market is huge, but an aspect of it which can be used effectively is the strong broker/agent network. This Startup Idea focuses on providing a platform for the brokers to exchange information about availability of real estate offerings and work in tandem for mutual benefit as a win-win solution rather than working in competition

- **SMS Based Healthcare for rural areas**

  - Considering low accessibility in rural areas, this platform can work on sms/call for providing health care services to people in rural areas as efficiently and on time as they are provided in urban areas

- **Alumni Connect**

  - A platform to allow any college to create a community for its alumni, not just for communication but also to see how they can contribute with their experience to the younger generation of their alma mater.

- **Real Estate Virtual Walkthrough**

  - This kind of app could really help people from anywhere to invest in real estate irrespective of their location. This is not about providing a standard video of the property, but an actual walkthrough by using Google Glass or other similar technology.

- **Agritech app/platform**

  - A platform to help agriculture efforts by using technology in activities like livestock monitoring, pest infiltration, soil/moisture/climatic data analytics for better yield.

Chapter 18

Trackschoolbus Starts Up – A Case Study

[Based on a very frequent request by many Startup Founders, here is a hypothetical Startup Case Study to illustrate the 7-Step Startup Success Formula]

"He is still not back from school. It's almost 4pm!", Rob panicked when he called his wife Jenny. Their son Jim, came back from school at 3pm everyday. It was 4pm and there was no sign of the school bus. Rob or Jenny didn't have the contact number of the school bus driver and neither were the kids allowed to take a cell phone to school. There was absolutely no trace! There were frantic calls from other parents who said the school had no idea too.

Amidst all the panic, suddenly the yellow gleaming school bus appeared on the driveway. There was a huge sense of relief. The driver said he had to fix a bad tire out of the blue and hence the delay.

Rob was a Software Developer. The geek in him immediately sprung to action. He decided he would create a mobile app which would allow tracing of the whereabouts of the school bus so that parents knew exactly where it was. And thus was born – TrackSchoolBus – Worry Free School Travel.

Startup Consultant Natalie

So, Rob had a brilliant idea on his hand. What next?

He decided to spend evenings and weekends after his day job to work on TrackSchoolBus. So, one fine Monday evening he sat down at his desk staring at a blank notebook but a whirlwind of thoughts inside his head. "So, I might need to hire 2 more developers if I have to do this in 2 months.. But then I don't have that much money…I'll create an impressive Pitch Deck and I'll approach investors…Wow! This is brilliant – I will also include a RFID feature which can scan the child's id card and report his boarding the bus to the parents".

It was a big jumble of all thoughts at one go. Rob felt he needed help. He decided to contact his friend Natalie who was a Startup Consultant.

Natalie assured Rob that there was a defined process that she had successfully implemented with other Startups. Following it to the T would help him achieve success in the timeframe that he desired.

Ground Work

Natalie and Rob met on a beautiful Saturday morning at a coffee shop. Natalie said "Rob, I don't mean to demotivate you. But here's the thing. Do you think TrackSchoolBus really has the potential that you think it has?" Rob was a little offended. After all this idea was so close to his heart.

Natalie took quite some time in making Rob understand that for every Startup Founder it was normal to feel this way. However, the smart thing to do, if he really wanted to make this happen, was to keep all sentiments aside and validate this idea.

Over the next few days, Natalie asked Rob to conduct surveys, list keywords related to his idea, and do some competitor research. Rob did as instructed and found out that he was not alone. There were others who had built such an app. He needed to add some "zing" to it to make it stand out. The good thing was that the survey reports clearly pointed out that there was a desperate need for something like that and that parents and schools were willing to pay if they had to but this would really take a load off their minds.

Once the groundwork was in place, Rob and Natalie decided to embark on the 7-Step Startup Success Formula Journey from the next day.

Step 1 – Document Your Vision

Natalie asked Rob some very focused questions. She asked him to randomly put down all the features that came to his mind for the TrackSchoolBus app. Then she asked him to hierarchically organise the thoughts and link them where appropriate. And thus was born the Mind Map

Then Natalie delved deeper. She asked Rob how he thought each feature would be represented in the app. She asked him to draw it on paper. There were a lot of back and forth revisions and finally Rob came up with a final Paper Prototype.

At this point Rob was highly excited. His vision had started becoming more and more tangible. It was time to give it the bells and whistles. The Logo was designed by outsourcing the job to a very efficient designer on Fiverr.

And then Natalie asked Rob the golden question. "What is it that zing that will distinguish you from your competitors?". And here Rob revealed his USP (Unique Selling Point) – "RFID tracker to ensure that my child boarded the bus or got off the bus".

Step 2 – Crafting your Team Vision

In the second meeting Rob raised a genuine concern. "Natalie, I did some calculations. I know that I will need at least 2 more developers if I have to create this app in the next 3 months. And if I get 3 developers, maybe I can develop some features in parallel and release the app in 2 months. And now comes the golden question – Should I hire these developers or should I outsource the requirement to freelancers or maybe a software development firm?"

"There is no defined answer for this which applies to all", Natalie said. "But there is a formula which can help you arrive at an answer. If you know that your product vision expands over a long term and also you will need many customisations since you cannot define everything right now, the answer is hire an in-house team. If your product vision is clearly defined and not dynamic in nature then outsource and get it done. There is a simple logic behind it – for every customisation that you ask for the outsourcing team will charge you separately. If you have too many customisations you might end up paying a lot and more importantly you might inhibit yourself thinking that every customisation that you ask for result in an expense."

Step 3 – Arranging for Funds needed to run the show

Rob decided to outsource work since he knew that the app had focused requirements and he knew exactly what he wanted based on the Paper Prototype and the Mind Map exercise that Natalie made him do.

The question was how to arrange for the money to hire these developers. And wait, he would need money for marketing too. Rob was a Software Developer. All this accounting jargon was mind boggling.

Natalie calmed him down and made him understand that it was just a matter of 2 documents.

One was the Financial Working Excel sheet. It was as simple as thinking of all Expenses – in Rob's case it was Web and app related hosting expenses, Software Development Expenses (which could be proposed by the Software Development Outsourcing team either as a Fixed Cost or Time and Material basis) and Marketing Expenses (which would be proposed by the Marketing Outsourcing team). For Marketing, Natalie made him understand basic metrics like CPC (Cost Per Click), CPL (Cost Per Lead). They identified the Revenue Model. They made some basic projections of the sales. Rob had the Expenses on one side, Project Revenue on the other side and the Financial Working Excel Sheet was ready. Of course, it would go through multiple iterations after brainstorming but the basic format was in place and that was good to go.

Now that the Financial ground work was done, it was a matter of putting everything that Rob had done till now – The Problem Definition, The Solution Definition and USP with high level figures of Expenses and Projected Revenue in an impressive presentation called the Pitch Deck.

Natalie connected him to Venture Capitalists who called Rob for various rounds of meetings. Finally, StellarStar Ventures saw the potential in the TrackSchoolBus app and pitched in to fund the venture.

It was a day of celebration!

Step 4 – Creating your Product

The initial Paper Prototype was in place and Rob was under the impression that it was enough to get things started off. He thought that all that needed to be done was handing over the Paper Prototype to the developers and telling them to get started off.

Natalie understood that like most other Startup Founders, Rob also wanted to see his dream come true ASAP. However, she sat him down and explained to him that to create a state-of-the-art product it was important to enter the end-user's mind and think like he did. And before that it was important to visualise your end-user as a real person, even give him/her a name so that he could visualise his actions better. This was the stage of User Persona definition and User Journey Planning.

Even though Rob had a clear picture of what he wanted in the app, Natalie explained to him that he needed to follow the Agile model of development. The focus would be to first define the MVP (Minimum Viable Product) and launch it. That would help in getting initial feelers. Then the next releases could be planned in phases. That way Go-To-Market time could be reduced.

Rob then handed over the User Persona, User Journey, Paper Prototype and Mind Map to the developers. Natalie instructed the developers to create a Static Prototype first. This is a clickable prototype which is not the real working product. It is just a series of pages with plain boxes and elements to give a tangible feel to the Paper Prototype.

Then came the part which took the most time, since presentation is the face of the app. The Development team had a UI/UX (User Interface/User Experience) specialist who focused on the look and feel of the app in terms of colours and layouts. He advised on changes in the User Journey to enrich the User Experience where he felt appropriate.

The Technical Architect created a technical model for the developers to follow and build the app. The choice of technology was of course based on the fact that it should not be obsolete and should allow a robust app which was scalable.

A perfect MVP was created based on the Paper Prototype and UI/UX framework. Finally, Rob realised his dream of the TrackSchoolBus app in a tangible form.

Step 5 – Convert Traffic to Leads

Once the product was ready, the next step was to tell the world about it. There is a lot of marketing jargon thrown around when a Startup starts outlining its marketing strategies. The best idea suggested by people is to just go out there on every possible social media channel and start talking about it.

Natalie skipped the jargon and explained to Rob that every social media channel has its own voice. Not every product can be marketed on every social media channel. You need to understand where your Target User Persona visits and focus only there to improve the chances.

Also, creating rich content which gives a clear message that you are the expert and you know what you are talking about is the key to drawing in the traffic. The keywords in the content will help Search Engines rank you better and show your content when people search for relevant keywords. That is Search Engine Optimisation (SEO). And yes, that is only half the battle won.

Once the traffic starts coming in, it is again upon you to provide value to the traffic. "Marketers call it Lead Magnets, I call it Value Magnet", Natalie explained. If your mission is to provide value to your end users, they will never hesitate in leaving behind an email id and allowing you to contact them in the future.

Funnelling that traffic into an email list of genuine users is the first stepping stone to your Startup Success.

Step 6 – Convert Leads to Sales

Once your Target Customer starts believing in you as the Expert and gives you the permission to connect to him, the Sales journey begins from there.

The Sales activity has a reputation which is not so good. Sales personnel are expected to nag, to keep calling their customers (sometimes at the most unearthly hours) to ensure they close a deal.

Natalie brought in a new perspective here – Marketing Automation.

If you really don't want to come across as "Salesy" use the advantages of email and SMS/Whatsapp communication. There are tools like Zoho and more who allow you to setup Automated Journeys where emails/sms are sent out automatically as per your preferences. Also, based on the user's action the further emails and sms are sent out in a customised manner which could be different for each user.

Natalie was quick to add here "I am not underplaying the effect of a Sales Call here. All that I am proposing here is that instead of making a Cold Call, it is better to bring the customer to a point where he knows you because you have been subtly knocking on his doors and then ask him if he is still interested. And well, even if he is not, he is there on your email list and he has allowed you to send him emails. If not today, then tomorrow maybe the need arises and he is ready just out of the blue to invest in your product."

So keep knocking subtly.

Step 7 – Serve Your Customer

Rob's TrackSchoolBus made much more revenue in the first month of its launch than they had projected. He was on top of the world.

At this point Natalie gave him some final sound advice. "Keep in touch with your customers all the time. All the more when they have a problem. Make sure you address problems first and then work on the future versions of your product. Serving your customer after you have made a sale will not only ensure longevity but also Word-Of-Mouth Referrals which are the biggest source for increasing your user base. And being the fan of Tools and Automation that I am, I would recommend using tools like Zoho Desk, Fresh Desk to take care of it for you so that you can serve them in an organised Ticketing Based System."

So, that was the Case Study of the Startup TrackSchoolBus from Idea to Profit using the 7-Step Startup Success Formula. Sincerely hope it does the same magic for you as it did for Rob.

Chapter 19

Startup Business Idea – Online Tuition Marketplace

Share The Love!

There are two kinds of entrepreneurs.

One, those who know what they want – they have a brilliant Startup Idea but don't know where to start. And then there are those, who really want to do create a Startup of their own, but don't have an idea that they feel is worth going ahead with.

This Blog Section – Startup Business Ideas – is dedicated to the second category. Call it a blessing if you may, but during my recreation time whenever I stare blankly outside my window, a Startup Idea starts creeping into my mind and doesn't stop pestering me till I write about it.

So here goes…

> *"Sometimes there is no better teacher than Crisis "*
> *– Anu Khanchandani*

The Inspiration

The inspiration is home born for this Startup Idea.

When the pandemic struck, my sister who is a reputed Tuition Teacher for Maths and Physics for Grade X onwards and Engineering students, found herself in confusion. The portion was half-way through and her students' careers were at stake. Here's a Pop quiz – To judge what needs to be done Right to achieve Unicorn Status.

We got into action and I created an online Learning Management System for her. Hadn't coded in years so I was a little jittery. WordPress and LearnPress with a few plugins here and there came to the rescue! I learnt it in a week and without any major coding whatsoever I created the Learning Management System (LMS) for her Institution.

The idea for Online Tuition MarketPlace originated from this. Here's the thing. If we can create this kind of setup for one teacher, why not extend it to an entire MarketPlace.

Why limit students to teachers only from local areas? Why not give a student an opportunity to learn from the best teachers around the world. And vice versa too. Why not give teachers the opportunity to achieve global expertise by giving them an opportunity to teach syllabi all across the world?

The Wish List

1. **Account Registration:** Teachers from all over the world can create profiles with their credentials and experience. Students from all over the world can create accounts and provide basic information about themselves in terms of location, grade etc.

2. **Choose Teacher:** Choose which teacher they want to learn from based on profile and experience and demo session. This option would be open in case they want to switch the teacher anytime during their course.

3. **Time Table :** For each class the student can specify suitable timings. Based on a combination of selected profiles and available times the system suggests a suitable teacher. A time table is generated for the entire year based on syllabus and selected timings.

4. **Course Packages** : The system accepts online payments via multiple payment gateways for convenience. There are multiple packages based on whether the student wants flexible timings or wants chat or video doubt sessions.

5. **Live Lectures** : Students attend lectures at designated times which were agreed upon during teacher selection.

6. **Anytime, Anywhere Course Material** : A centralised location at which all recorded lectures and notes are uploaded for anytime access.

7. **Tests :** Teachers can conduct multiple choice or subjective exams periodically. Students can submit their answer papers online which will be checked by the teacher in the same place and grades will be notified to the student.

8. **Doubt Sessions** : The student can set up Doubt Sessions with the teacher at agreed times. Doubt sessions could be chat/video based on Payment Packages.

9. **Open Forum** : The student can have chat/video discussions with peers from all across the world.

This wish list includes only the initial thoughts. I'm sure if you are genuinely interested to create this kind of a global teaching platform, as we brainstorm, more useful features will come up.

The Unique Selling Proposition(s)

There are many such platforms in India – the prime ones being Byju's , Vedantu and many more have sprung up in the past year. The USP that we can offer through this Startup Idea is that it is global, it doesn't bind the student to a fixed time table proposed by the governing platform. The student is free to choose a teacher of his/her own preference, with the option of working out a suitable time between both of them.

Bottomline, the students have a right to choose – be it time table, be it teacher and is not limited to a local choice – the world is open for choosing the teacher that they think is best for them.

Where will the money come from?

- Commission from Course Packages based on
  - Teacher Expertise
  - Chat/Video Doubt Sessions
- Advertisements from related vendors like Book Sellers

What kind of expenses are we looking at?

- Website/Blog/LMS Setup – Approximately Rs. 20000/- (One-Time)
- Domain and Hosting – Approximately Rs. 5000/- (Yearly)
- Zoom for Live Classes – Approximately Rs. 15000/- (Yearly)

Chapter 20

Startup Business Idea – Interior Design App

Share The Love!

The inspiration

One of the most tedious activities a couple has to go through is a home shift. It is tedious in a practical way but for sure there is also an associated excited flutter in your heart where you visualise a new life with your family. I thought I had it all settled in my mind that I needed xyz and abc to set up a new life. But slowly and gradually the pqr, lmn started adding up as things started coming to my mind. Right from a flower vase to a custom closet, my mind was soon bogged down by the amount of activities I had to manage related to home shifting. I did manage eventually using an Evernote list but decided in my mind that I would create an app to help others do this more effectively and yeah why not make some name, fame and fortune for myself too. Caught up in the daily grind I still haven't had the time to do it (like the many other ideas that I had thought of earlier) so here I am throwing out all my thoughts to the developer community out there to give shape to my dream.

The wish list

- Will help people who have bought a new home/office to set it up in an organized way right from deciding what they want to do in it to finding the right vendors to get it done

- App elements

  - Home/Office Organizer

    - Deciding elements of work

    - Organizing elements of work by room e.g. set up a lounger in the dining area

- - Organizing elements of work by category of work e.g. civil, electric, carpentry etc
- Keep the purse strings tight
  - Give estimations as per your knowledge to arrive at a budget
- Choose the right vendor (Possibility of using Data Science here)
  - Vendor Listing with details
  - Vendor quotations
  - Share quotations
  - Compare quotations
  - Check out other vendors
    - Focused shopping – with similar products as you want
    - The full mall – all products by all vendors
- Pick and choose
  - Existing Template designs with estimation
- Live your design
  - Visualise design – Upload your home pics/plan layout and place elements and see how it looks
  - 3D view (Augmented Reality)
- Wishlist(Possibility of using Data Science here)
  - The app will find vendors who provide whats on your wishlist
- FavoritesCollection

- - Create a collection of favorite pics from which you can shortlist finally to create your home elements
  - Expert Advice
  - Color Palette
    - Complete Color Palette
    - Click and choose
- Revenue plan
  - Ads by vendors
  - Interior designers
    - for expert advice
    - for putting up their portfolio
- Similar apps
  - https://play.google.com/store/apps/details?id=com.houzz.app
  - https://play.google.com/store/apps/details?id=fr.anuman.HomeDesign3D
  - https://play.google.com/store/apps/details?id=com.zalebox.living.room.decorating.ideas.s1&hl=en
  - https://www.androidauthority.com/best-home-design-apps-home-improvement-apps-android-799037/
  - http://joyofandroid.com/best-home-design-apps-for-android/
  - https://www.1stdibs.com/blogs/the-study/interior-design-apps/

- Edge
  - Not many apps like this. Do have features like home visualisation etc. but not organizer, vendor co-ordination
- Expenses
  - App
  - Website
  - Blog
  - Digital Marketing

Chapter 21

What is Startup Success After All?!

Share The Love!

The Oxford definition of Success – "The accomplishment of an aim or purpose". Just below this in a bullet point it is quick to add – " The attainment of fame, wealth, or social status."

I was slightly shocked and amused at the same time to read this quick addition! Success is a very broad term and often relates to the context which we are referring it in. Success to a student is totally a different story compared to what success means to maybe an athlete. What I am talking about here today is Professional Success. In the past 2 decades after having stunts of being in and out of this corporate jungle, having met various types of professionals , I may not be a maestro at this but I think I am capable enough to express my opinions on what professional success should actually be. What needs to be done and more importantly... not done ... to make sure you are at least close if not there completely. A few pointers based on my journey and experience ...

What professional success is usually judged by :

* A huge turnover

* Large number of Human Resources

* Plush Offices all across the geography

* CEO invited to important conferences

* Capacity of the organisation to have a huge marketing budget which allows it to have sprawling ads in the most popular dailies

* IPO Listing!

And so on and so forth ...

Having worked for all types and sizes of companies from the dingiest of rooms to the swankiest of skyscrapers.. to working from home for someone somewhere in a remote area of Portugal… I feel privileged to have seen it all! And looking back, the best times were ….when I was going clickety-clicking on my keyboard, sitting comfortably on a swing in my balcony coding in a new programming language I had just learnt .. as a consultant to a client abroad whom I had never seen, just spoken on the phone .. I think my most successful achievement as a professional was that project which I did as a single professional for a single entrepreneur. There was no big organisational entity anywhere, there were no plush offices, there was no huge turnover but there was a huge consultant fee which was mine and only mine for the keeps !! This client's word of mouth recommendations got me more work, adulation and money. I also had the comfort of working for my own self, in the organised way that I want. For me that was professional success.. a job well done!

So then, why is it that the world defines success by plush offices and large turnovers (which are actually zero profits). I am not changing the definition of the world here, but what I am trying to bring to the book is that success goes deeper than that! Yes, all the tangible material aspects of success are important to boost one's morale but just that without certain core elements cannot and should not be defined as success. Some of the core elements according to me ..

* Client appreciation.. a pat on your back ..... not just a client testimonial . A testimonial which comes from the heart, not because you have requested him that you would come to his place on a day or time and he should speak good about you since you need it to boost your business

* Happy employees who not only talk good about you on your face but behind your back to others. They don't call you a mentor .. they treat you as a role model and imitate you unknowingly . They don't have to be forced to work overnight or on weekends, they do it themselves coz they love what they do

* Systematic processes in each element of your work . Unorganised work ultimately reflect clearly on the end result !

* Sensible business expenditures. Frugality for your own self , never for your employees. I would rather have one employee less rather than having a ton, but being able to give them the employee welfare that they so deserve.

* Constant learning and training yourself and your colleagues. Ad-hoc sessions over the day in a coffee shop more than formal expensive inductions

* Accepting new changes and imbibing them on your organisational culture. You won't have to force your people to adopt them, they will love to do it coz they know their personal growth is associated with it too !

* Talking less and being a role model by rolling up your sleeves once in a while and getting down to the grind with your people to show them how it's done.. by being a living example than just being a motivational speaker

* Sometimes letting your employees make mistakes and learn is the best way to teach them something

* Micromanage or not – that's been an age old debate which managers of the universe can't stop talking enough about. My mantra after a lot of learning and observing- if things seem to go fine, there is no need to micromanage. But if things are going on a roller coaster ride, time to roll up those sleeves again and get to the root of the problem. At all times, keep out a watchful eye for systems and processes broken to achieve deadlines. Nip these practices in the bud so that they don't become a habit. That way they are not broken .. not because they know that there is a lurking watchful eye but because not breaking them has become a habit.

At the end of it all, my strong feeling says that if you do these things right , the plush offices , high profits, IPO listings will just fall into your lap. The vision and the mission should be setting these small things right .. the cliches will happen automatically as an after effect of these small things set right! But getting IPO listings without these small important elements in place will be success as the world defines it … but not what you know deep down inside as success. Superficial success – yes! But spiritual success – No!

Work for a cause.. not applause

Live a life to express ..not to impress

Don't strive to make your presence felt ..

Do things that make your absence felt

And that my friend will be a real success !!!

Afterword

Hope I was able to encapsulate my journey of 25 years into this bundle in an efficient way.

Hope you take up the 7-steps towards your startup success one-by-one. In case you need hand-holding I am just an email away - anu@thegreycells.com.

Also, it is my passion to listen to early-stage startup stories and challenges and hand-hold them in any way that I can. Feel free to book an appointment https://links.thegreycells.com/BookAppointment

If you really enjoyed this book and want to enrol in a one-on-one workshop where I guide you through your Startup Journey and hand-hold you along the 7-steps on video and with workshops (which you can send me and I will assess them and revert to you) , do check out https://thegreycells.com/wordpress-cms/product/startup-idea-to-business-plan-in-60-days/

Get the ball rolling and get into action towards making your Startup "THE NEXT BIG THING"

Here's a little something from Warren Buffet to get you started off :

I don't look to jump over 7-foot bars - I look for 1-foot bars that I can step over.

-Warren Buffet, Berkshire Hathaway chairman and CEO

About the Author

An engineer, entrepreneur and coach for the past 25 years, Anu Khanchandani has been contributing as a Digital Professional in various roles across her career. With a plethora of experience across MNCs and Startups alike, she has taken efforts to provide her experience and the expertise gained along the way as a Software Developer, Project Manager, Agile Coach, Principal Mentor to all organisations she has been a part of.

She conceptualised a disruptive Fintech - Fintoo (www.fintoo.in) - from scratch since 2015 as a Co-Founder and heads the Digital Initiatives of the company with a team of 50 Digital Professionals.

After having spent more than 25 years as an Employee, Coach and Consultant in the Digital Startup industry in India and abroad she saw the journey and the challenges faced during it. Be it product design, marketing, selling, funding each aspect of the journey needed to be taken up carefully – planned and executed with patience rather than rushing into it blindfolded.

That is when she founded The Grey Cells (www.thegreycells.com) which is a Startup Incubator.

She has been a part of the following startups as a mentor, coach and consultant :

- Coodle (Baby Gear Rental - ECommerce)

- Bharat Credit - (Online Loan Advisor)

- Mad About Sports - (Sports Edtech)

- Mrigavya Organic - (Organic Products D2C - Ecommerce)

- Vahanom - (Online Automobile Service)

- Properative - (Real Estate Advisory)

  and many more..

As part of The Grey Cells, she aims to provide an Online Incubator for Startups which offers consulting, coaching and training – only because she believes that it is time to give back to the Digital World what it has taught her in the past 25 years.